worldviews

THINK FOR YOURSELF ABOUT HOW YOU SEE GOD

**Written by John M. Yeats
and John Blase
General Editor Mark Tabb**

TH1NK
P.O. Box 35001
Colorado Springs, Colorado 80935

TH1NK is an imprint of NavPress.

TH1NK and the TH1NK logo are registered trademarks of NavPress. Absence of ® in connection with marks of NavPress or other parties does not indicate an absence of registration of those marks.

ISBN 1-57683-955-9

Cover design by Arvid Wallen
Creative Team: Nicci Hubert, Karen Lee-Thorp, Erika Hueneke, Kathy Mosier, Bob Bubnis

Yeats, John M.
 Worldviews think for yourself about how we see God / written by John
M. Yeats and John Blase ; general editor, Mark Tabb.
    p. cm. -- (TH1NK reference collection)
 Includes bibliographical references.
 ISBN 1-57683-955-9
 1. Christianity and other religions. 2. Religions. 3.
Religions--Philosophy. 4. Religion--Philosophy. 5. Spirituality. I.
Blase, John. II. Tabb, Mark A. III. Title. IV. Series.
 BR127.Y43 2006
 261.2--dc22
                              2006011191

Printed in the United States of America

1 2 3 4 5 6 7 8 9 10 / 10 09 08 07 06

FOR A FREE CATALOG OF NAVPRESS BOOKS & BIBLE STUDIES,
CALL 1-800-366-7788 (USA) OR 1-800-839-4769 (CANADA)

Contents

About the TH1NK
REFERENCE COLLECTION

The TH1NK REFERENCE COLLECTION isn't an ordinary set of reference books. Like all of the books in the TH1NK line, we wrote these books for students. That doesn't mean we inserted some hip language into an otherwise dry, boring book to try to make it sound with it and cool, dude. Instead, we built these books on a couple of assumptions about you.

First, we knew you want honest representations of various points of view. Although all the books in the REFERENCE COLLECTION are written from an evangelical Christian position, we didn't dismiss all other viewpoints. Instead, we wrote these books in such a way that those holding different worldviews and theological perspectives would be able to read these books and say, *Yes, this gives a good outline of what I and others believe.* To assure theological balance, all of the books in this collection have been reviewed by a panel of scholars from various theological perspectives and academic fields (see page 228 for a list of those scholars).

We also believed you are able to draw your own conclusions. Whether the question regards what Buddhists believe or whether Christians can lose their salvation, we didn't connect all the dots for you. Each book presents several perspectives. You will have to take the next step on your own and figure out what you believe and why you believe it. Our goal is to do more than answer questions. The TH1NK REFERENCE COLLECTION is designed to make you think through your own beliefs and convictions, as well as those of others.

Finally, we assumed you want something more than a place to turn for answers to your questions about Islam or Psalm 119 or the role of women in the church. That's why we designed these books to be read, not just used for research. You can read them from cover to cover. Along the way, you will find that these books not only dispense information but also entertain you and challenge you and the way you see your world.

Mark Tabb
General Editor

A Collapsible House

Dust. That was all that remained of Valentina's home. All her life she'd lived in the same building in St. Petersburg, Russia. Now it was nothing but rubble. Unknown to Valentina and the 490 other residents of the apartment building, their home had been sinking slowly for weeks. Just beneath the surface, a leaking water main steadily washed away the soil under the foundation.

One summer morning Valentina sat enjoying her morning cup of coffee when the whole building started to shake. She ran to the front door of her apartment and flung it open. Instead of a hallway, she found herself looking out over empty space, space filled with nothing but dust.

Over time, the water leaking from the water main had made the foundation unstable. It was only a matter of time before the building could no longer support its own weight. Gravity always wins.

To state the obvious, any building without a solid foundation is doomed to collapse.

Jesus knew a thing or two about buildings and foundations. In the parable of the builders, he said anyone who obeys his teachings builds on a solid foundation.[1] When storms come, the house stands firm because it is anchored to the rock. But the foolish builder puts his house on the sand. The beach location is great, but when the storms come, the sand washes out the foundation and the house collapses. Both builders exerted the same amount of time and energy in building, but in the end, the house with the weak foundation doesn't last.

TRADING A ROCK FOR SHIFTING SAND

The sand washed out from under my world, sending it crashing down, one Thursday afternoon. I didn't lose my home like Valentina. No one died, nor did anyone lose his material possessions. Instead, my world collapsed because of ideas. And it was seismic, to say the least.

I grew up in a Christian home, accepted Christ at a young age, and generally stayed out of trouble. When I went off to college I continued to practice my faith, but I began to soften my positions on certain issues here and there. The more I read, the more ideas I encountered. Instead of checking them against the Bible, I simply accepted them. They sounded good and made sense. After all, the people writing my textbooks had to know more than I did, right?

I left college and headed to Oxford to work on my first graduate degree. After weeks of papers and exams, my first term was nearly over, and I started counting the days until Christmas break. That's when the building started to shake. While sketching the outline for a critical review of another book, I suddenly realized I had a problem. A very serious problem. The weight of the ideas I'd collected over the past few years began to take its toll. I was a Christian, but when I took these ideas to their logical end, my Christianity no longer made sense.

This confrontation between my faith and the ideas I accepted during my university years confused me. I never saw this conflict coming. I had already integrated these ideas with my faith. Or so I thought. In that moment of realization, it was as if my entire foundation was swept away and my worldview collapsed. In many ways, I felt as if I had a choice: either abandon Christianity, or abandon my current philosophy of life.

Over the next few months, I analyzed and evaluated everything I believed. I realized the ideas that had seemed so impressive in college were not congruent with a Christian perspective on life. Even though I had tried to make them mesh with my Christianity, they had slowly eroded my foundation for life. I'd traded my rock-solid foundation for sand. The more I accepted worldly wisdom, the more beach sand I bought. Although the view was good for a while, when the storm finally hit, my house collapsed.

I'd like to say this problem was easy to fix. Instead, it took lots of hard work. I had to revisit just about everything I believed. Who was God? What did I believe about the Bible? Who was Jesus? To some people, sorting through every idea in my head sounds crazy. To me, it was the most important thing I could possibly do. I needed to know what I believed and why. This was not a task I could do by myself. If I had tried to analyze everything on my own, I would have missed something. Instead, my road to rebuilding my worldview had two main components.

First, I sorted out what I believed about the Bible. In order to nail that down, I spent lots of time reading and praying. I asked God to reveal to me what he said about life. If I was going to truly evaluate Christianity, I needed to know the sourcebook of the faith.

Second, I found someone I could talk to. This was the harder challenge. I wanted someone who would be brutally honest with me. A friend of mine, Doug, was willing to dialogue with me as I sought answers. Every time I contemplated one issue or another, he asked key questions that helped me take my ideas to their logical conclusions. He also helped me see the places where what I was thinking didn't match the other things

I believed. Without someone older and wiser than me serving as a sounding board for my ideas, it would have been very difficult to get back on track.

This book will help you sort through your belief system, just as I had to sort through mine. As you read, you need to do three things. First, keep your Bible handy. If I make a statement about the Bible or Christian faith that you're not sure of, look up the passage I reference or see what you can find in your Bible on that subject. Also, see what the Bible says about the ideas of other worldviews. If you don't feel you're enough of a Bible expert to do this, that leads to my second suggestion: Find a mentor with whom you can discuss the ideas you find here. Finally, and most importantly, think as you read. This book is simply an attempt to help you build on the solid foundation of Jesus Christ and understand the very different foundations others build on. With all the world's philosophies, religions, and ideas, it's hard to know which concepts you should accept as true and which are incompatible with the claims of Christianity. As we walk together through the maze of dominant worldviews, I hope this book will help you maintain a focus on Christ in a confusing world.

A SCENIC TOUR

My family traveled a lot when I was a kid. Some of my favorite stops on each road trip were the scenic overlooks. These overlooks gave me a sense of the grandeur of nature and let me get a bird's-eye view of the landscape. However, they didn't let me see everything close-up. To do that, my dad had to stop the car and let my brother and me get out and explore. He did that occasionally, but most of the time we had to hurry down the road to get to our destination.

Each of the worldviews we will discuss in this book will be like a scenic overlook. We'll give you the most important points you need to know about each, but we won't have enough space to explore each one in great detail.

YOUR WORLDVIEW ROAD MAP

Most maps offer a legend that helps you understand the symbols used for interstates, airports, national forests, and points of interest. Similarly, to gain our bearings in each worldview, six items will appear on the legend of our worldview road map. We will take an overview of the history and major ideas of a worldview and then examine the following points of interest:

1. *God.* Every worldview believes something about God, even if it doesn't believe he exists. We will explore these beliefs and the way the worldview being examined handles the concept of God.

2. *Humanity.* Did an intelligent Creator make human beings, or are they the end result of time plus chance? Do they have any moral responsibility in the universe? What is each person's place in the world? Because people are the ones who follow ideas, all worldviews answer these questions in different ways.

3. *Salvation.* If your car breaks down on your way to Yosemite Valley, who will come to the rescue? What about when things break down in your universe? Who, or what, if anything, comes to your aid? We will explore what each view has to say about salvation and redemption for human beings.

4. *Authority.* No one wants to talk about authority, but we can't live without it. Every worldview acknowledges some form of authority. Whether a divine book, human reason, human emotion, or even science, something makes rules and gives ultimate answers to life's biggest questions. Whatever a worldview sets as its authority anchors its logical framework and gives boundaries to its beliefs.

5. *Time.* Time is always marching on. We humans become major casualties in the battle against time, so time is relevant to every worldview. It addresses questions such as, What is the purpose of existence? and What happens after death?

6. *Jesus.* Jesus asked Peter, "Who do you say I am?" We will pose this question to every worldview. Who does it say Jesus is?

We will explore each of these six issues within each chapter. The Worldview Legend on pages 212–219 provides a summary of the six issues for all of the worldviews. This chart will help you differentiate between the various worldviews at a glance. You can also use it to compare the different views to Christianity.

THE LAST FEW ADJUSTMENTS

Remember, every trip you take has a few challenging moments. This one is no different. You will soon encounter ideas that will challenge ideas you've held for a very long time. This book is designed to help you think through these issues that every person faces. The big payoff comes in the end. By the time you finish this book, you will know much more about what you believe and why. As you listen to teachers, watch movies, or interact with peers, you will begin to be able to discern the viewpoints they are communicating. And you will have the skills to check those worldviews against your own.

Nothing in this book is new. Three thousand years ago Solomon wrote, "There is nothing new under the sun."[2] Because all of these ideas have been around for a long time, many of them have names that have been assigned by some thinker at some point in history. Many of those words are "isms": naturalism, materialism, humanism. We will introduce you to these terms and carefully explain what they are. And at the end of each chapter, you will find a glossary of key terms in case any are unclear.

If you haven't picked up on it yet, let's be clear about the viewpoint of this book's authors. We believe that the message of the Bible is the only foundation for a true, solid worldview that is anchored in teachings that have stood the test of time. The Bible is not just some book, but is literally God's Word. We also believe that if all Christians lived according to a fully Christian worldview, the world around us would be a different place. Because we hold this to be true, we will start with an introduction to a Christian worldview before we move on to discuss alternate perspectives. However, although we feel strongly that the biblical worldview is the true one, we intend to present the other worldviews with full respect. If you show this book to a friend who is a naturalist or a Buddhist, for example, we hope they will feel we have represented their outlook fairly.

Are you ready?

What Is a Worldview?

The term *worldview* is adapted from a German word that means a "perspective or outlook on the world."[1] When we talk about your worldview, we are referring to your perspective on life. Put another way, your worldview is the filter that helps you make sense of your experiences and the reality around you.

Perhaps an illustration would help: I have astigmatism. This means the shape of my eye does not allow light to hit the correct portion of my cornea. I have to strain the muscles in my eyes to correct this problem, which in turn gives me bad headaches. After years of eyestrain headaches, I finally went to see an optometrist. He prescribed glasses that reshape the direction of the light so I can see clearly without straining my eyes. Even better, my headaches are long gone.

Your worldview is like the lenses in my glasses. It filters every event, every experience, and everything you learn so you can interpret and organize this barrage of information into a holistic view of the world. Your worldview shapes the way you live and encompasses what you believe. And, just as the lenses in my glasses need a frame to hold them in place in front of my eyes, the lens of your worldview needs a supportive framework, or a foundation, to keep it in place.

WHO HAS A WORLDVIEW?

As long as you have a pulse and your brain is working, you have a worldview, whether you realize it or not. There is no escape. You have probably heard people talk about "finding themselves." It's not as if their body got lost and they set out to find it again. Instead, they are discovering or rediscovering their worldview. Somehow, in the course of time, their old lenses for filtering reality collapsed. They had to start over and find new frameworks and new lenses. But the more they try new ones on, the more confused they become. They wander in and out of different religions and philosophies trying to find something that will help them make sense of their world. Eventually they will land somewhere and construct some form of a framework on which they will operate.

You can't function without a worldview. The way you live—your choices, decisions, and direction—is bound up in your worldview. *To discover your worldview is to discover who you are.*

HOW DID I GET A WORLDVIEW?

Your worldview came to you from many different sources. The way you interpret reality was shaped by your family, the media, your religion (or lack thereof), education (or lack thereof), friends, experiences, community, and everything else that crosses your path. Your view of the world began the moment your life began. In the womb, all you knew was the comfort of a heartbeat and the muffled voice of your mother. After birth, your horizons continually expanded: from the crib to the play-pen, to your whole house, to the backyard, and to the neighborhood park. The day you started school or joined your first sports team, you learned you weren't the center of the universe. To get along, you had to share, communicate, and control your temper. Your world as a child expanded as you learned the basic rules that are part of everyone's life: You should always tell the truth, you should share, and your actions actually do affect someone besides yourself.

As you mature and read, learn, and experience new things, your worldview has to accommodate. The experience of traveling outside of your city, state, or even home country for the first time changes how you relate to the world around you. Without a solid foundation as a part of your worldview, you risk drifting aimlessly in the sea of "Who am I really?" In the pages that follow, we hope to help you anchor your worldview on the solid rock of biblical, orthodox Christianity while making you aware of competing worldviews.

HOW DOES A WORLDVIEW WORK?

As you encounter life, there are things you learn on a day-by-day basis. For example, you learned early in life that gravity exists—even before you knew what gravity was from a scientific perspective. It only took one or two falls off of the back of the sofa for you to figure out how it worked. In the process, you also discovered that landing on a cushion is much better than landing on a hard floor!

But a worldview is much more than experientially learned data. As you read, listen to teachers, or watch TV, thoughts and concepts confront you, and you don't always understand how to deal with them. Your worldview becomes the framework by which you can interpret this new data and decide what to do with it. This process is called critical thinking.

Here's how it works. Imagine you're watching a special about the Egyptian pyramids on your favorite channel. In school you learned the pharaohs ordered the construction of the pyramids some 4,500 years ago. You have a general idea of where they are, and you may have even visited them at some point in your life. In other words, you know quite a bit of data about the pyramids. As you are watching this television special, the host asks who built these architectural wonders. He clicks off the usual suspects: famous kings, slave laborers, or the children of Israel. The host then argues that the mathematical precision used in building the pyramids proves that no human could have built them. Instead, he contends a master race of aliens came along and built these giant monuments that the Egyptian kings eventually used as burial sites. The host parades an endless line of so-called experts to prove his point.

As a viewer, with the data you already know, you can respond to this program's new insight in one of three ways:

1. You turn off the TV or change channels because this show just left the galaxy of reality. You may not believe in aliens, or the argument just doesn't make sense, but either way, you choose to *screen out* the data you are presented.

2. You finish watching the show. You may keep watching because you find the host's ideas so absurd that they are spectacularly funny. Or, you may want to keep watching because you find his presentation intriguing. After the show is over, you *judge* the data presented. How do the arguments compare to what you already know? Why would such an argument be presented at all? Who financed the show? Who were the so-called experts? In the end, you may choose to screen out the data as absurd — do aliens exist at all? — after thinking through the show's ideas in light of what you know.

3. You finish watching the show. You become so engrossed in the presentation that you never think that the host might have an agenda. In fact, unknown to you, the show was financed and produced by the Aliens Are Everywhere Society, an organization whose sole purpose is to try to convince you that aliens exist. The program, its graphics, and the "experts" who testified to the validity of the argument have you convinced. You *simply*

accept the data presented as fact, and you begin believing not only that aliens exist, but also that they built the pyramids.

If you choose the first option, your worldview may be prompting you to change the channel. The idea that aliens exist is so far removed from what you know and believe that to continue watching the program would simply be a waste of time.

Let's say you choose the second option. You watch the program and begin to ask critical questions. After the show, you do a quick Internet search on the names of the "experts" and find out they are plumbers and bricklayers who use their spare time to research the paranormal. These are not the sort of people you would necessarily trust for your final decisions about the origins of the pyramids. You check the name of the producer and discover that he is the founder of the Aliens Are Everywhere Society, a group you know to be untrustworthy. In the end, you arrive at the same conclusion as the first option. You screen out the data since there is nothing worthwhile in it.

However, you may feel lazy when the program comes on, and the batteries in your remote are dead. So you watch the entire show. Instead of thinking through the program, however, you simply choose to watch the show and turn off your worldview filters. You miss that the people presented as experts really aren't. You don't compare any data from the show with what you already know to be true. In the end, you accept everything in the show without thinking. You store a file away in your brain that says aliens exist and they built the pyramids. Let's also assume that you are a Christian. At no point does it cross your mind that perhaps the concept of aliens involved in human history runs counter to your belief in God and his special plan for humanity.

Would believing that aliens built the pyramids really threaten your entire worldview? Probably not. But let's say you're sitting in a biology class at college and the professor begins to argue that the earth did not evolve but was made by a superior alien race. Hmmm. Your brain clicks back to that show you watched on aliens and pyramids. Somehow things begin to make sense. In fact, with the data the professor begins to put forward, you are overwhelmed with the scientific proofs he presents and decide that your belief that God created the universe seems so naive. Perhaps the aliens were the creators after all . . .

We know this is a ridiculous illustration, but later in this book we'll talk about specific worldviews that are much more convincing. You need to know what you believe and why. You also need to think critically about what you hear and check it against the ultimate standard of your life. Failure to evaluate information through the lenses of a Christian worldview can erode the foundations of what you believe and lead you to a life of contradictions.

WHAT IF MY WORLDVIEW IS DIFFERENT FROM SOMEONE ELSE'S?

What happens when your worldview is different from your friend Cathy's? Let's say the two of you visit a local art museum and study Monet's famous painting "Water Lilies." Cathy may comment on Monet's use of color that gives the painting depth. The two of you begin to look closely at the colors. Cathy, an avid fan of the color blue, starts arguing with you over the exact shade of blue Monet used. Is it navy? Aquamarine? Sky blue? At the end of the conversation, you both agree that Monet used blue, but the slight shadings lead you to disagree over the specifics. If my father, who is color-blind, had been standing next to the two of you, he would have brought a completely different perspective to the discussion.

Even though you may find points of contact with other people whose perspectives of the world are similar to yours, you will still have disagreements at times because we all see things differently. The question is, are these just minor differences (blue can have different shades and still be blue), or are there chasms between your worldview and others' (red and green are not the same color even though they look the same shade of gray to my father)?

This poses a problem. If there are so many perspectives, how can any one view be right? According to many people today, it's okay to believe whatever you want, because in the end, all that matters is that it works for you. Many people sincerely believe that everyone's beliefs are equally valid on all levels. They call it "tolerance," to make sure that everyone accepts any worldview that someone else might believe. This idea is bizarre to me. Everyone has a worldview, but there are fundamental issues at the heart of each worldview that conflict with other perspectives. Now, this doesn't mean there should be a Worldview War I. Instead, we can learn to respect other worldviews, even though there will always be some level of disagreement.

For Christians, this is especially important. What the Bible teaches about truth and Christ is sometimes considered offensive to other people. How do we handle this? Let's step back to the optometrist's office for a moment. When I went to my appointment to have my eyes checked, there was a definite problem with my vision. I tried to read the eye exam chart, but I couldn't make out all of the letters. In fact, the letters were so blurry that I mistook the letter *G* for the letter *C*. Even if I believed with all my heart that it really was the letter *C* on the chart, would that change the fact that it was actually *G*? No. I needed something to correct my vision. There was a right answer, but until the appropriate lens dropped in front of my eyes, I could have gone on thinking that a *C* was a *G*.

The worldview of a Christian is vastly different from that of someone who is a Muslim, a naturalist, or a materialist. Christians, Muslims, and materialists agree that there are answers to life's big questions. And we disagree in important, substantive ways about what the answers are. Those disagreements matter, and they can't be swept under a rug of "tolerance." We can agree to disagree and live alongside one another peacefully, but that isn't the same as saying the differences don't matter.

Christians believe that the only way to see and understand the answers to life's big questions is by looking through the right lens: the Bible. God's Word illuminates the truth God offers to all of humanity. Just as the lenses in my glasses give me 20/20 vision so I can see clearly, so also the Bible gives us 20/20 vision about life. We will talk more about this when we discuss Christianity in the next section.

Of course, no Christian individual or group is right about everything. The Bible is infallible, but our interpretations are limited. Sometimes we get things wrong, and there's room for disagreement about details. Just as you can disagree with your friend Cathy about Monet's exact shade of blue—while agreeing that it's blue and not purple—so Christians can disagree about the details of life's questions while agreeing on the basics.

This matter of the Bible returns us to fundamental questions about the foundation of our worldview. At the base of every worldview is a simple assumption about authority. When all else fails, who is in charge? For a Christian, the answer is that the authority for our lives is God and his Word. For a Muslim, it is the teachings of Muhammad and the Koran. For a naturalist or materialist, it is the individual. You can probably imagine that because these groups have different authorities, their worldviews will clash, perhaps even fiercely. You shouldn't expect people with different worldviews to be on the same page as you. This book will give you a starting place for understanding the basics of the Christian worldview and other views as well. Over time you'll want to investigate these ideas more fully, but this volume represents a starting point for your engagement of the culture around you. Before we continue, however, there is one last question.

CAN A WORLDVIEW BE CHANGED?

Yes. This is why we must continually evaluate everything we take in from the world around us. Other worldviews are in competition for your heart and mind. As teachers, there is nothing that discourages us more than to see a student become attracted to some element of a competing worldview and end up buying into the whole picture without looking carefully at its flaws. There are reasons why thoughtful Christians have considered and rejected certain ideas. There are reasons why Christians have maintained other ideas throughout centuries of the culture's changing seasons. The Christian worldview isn't rooted in ignorance of other views, but in careful reflection on how the world actually is.

Some students come back to their faith later down the road, but many don't. The foundations of their Christian worldview slowly erode away and are replaced by elements from some other worldview. In an attempt to be internally consistent, these students jettison more and more aspects of the Christian perspective to create room for their new philosophies. The process accelerates when the person immerses himself in a community that shares his new belief.

But just as some people gradually shift away from the Christian worldview, so others gradually shift toward it. For years, Antony Flew firmly held his title as atheist. He debated Christians and other theists in an attempt to convince them of their wrong-headed thinking. Gary Habermas, a professor at Liberty University, often served as a sparring partner with Flew. The two debated one another publicly at both Christian and non-Christian universities. Over time, they built a strong relationship even though they disagreed sharply over the reality of God. As they continued to dialogue with each other for almost twenty years, Flew examined Christianity more closely. Finally, in 2004, he admitted publicly that he had shifted his position. He was no longer an atheist, but a theist.

Although Flew accepts no specific religious tradition, such as Christianity or Judaism, he did change his worldview to accept a very broad understanding of God. As an atheist, he continued to study and read and eventually realized that his humanistic explanations were insufficient. For him, science demanded that there must be some designer of the universe, and he embraced theism. His basic worldview changed on a fundamental level from denial of God to acceptance that a god exists.[2]

The apostle Paul tells the church in Corinth that when we accept Christ as our Savior, we are a new creation. All of the old things pass away and everything is made new.[3] Paul is talking about a major shift in a person's outlook on the world, a shift that reflects the reality of the cross of Christ. In a word, he describes a change of worldviews.

WHY DO I NEED TO KNOW THIS STUFF?

There are several reasons why you ought to know about your worldview and the worldviews of others. As we've already said, discovering your worldview is finding out who you are. Likewise, discovering other people's worldviews is finding out who they are. Then, when you hear people talk about life or watch movies or just engage with those around you, you'll know where other people are coming from. G. K. Chesterton, a famous philosopher and journalist, told his readers that "the most practical and important thing about a man is still his view of the universe."[4] Why would this be important?

Think of it this way: If a worldview determines identity, and if everyone on the planet has a worldview, for you and me to even know someone, we must know his or her worldview. Chesterton wrote:

> We think that for a general about to fight an enemy, it is important to know the enemy's numbers, but still more important to know the enemy's philosophy. We think the question is not whether the theory of the cosmos affects matters, but whether in the long run, anything else affects them.[5]

Chesterton was right. There is nothing more important than a person's view of the universe. Worldview is crucial for understanding ourselves and each other.

SCENIC OVERLOOK AHEAD!

We have arrived at our first scenic overlook. Are you ready? In this first overlook, we will be focusing on the Christian worldview. This is the best place to start so you know where you stand as a Christian. Before we exit, please remember: Everyone has a worldview. You cannot function as a human without one. The way your life is lived — your choices, decisions, and direction — is bound up in your worldview. To discover your worldview is to discover who you are.

Christianity

Introduction to Christianity
God
Humanity
Salvation
Authority
Time
Jesus

*"I am the way, the truth, and the life.
No one can come to the Father except
through me."*

— JESUS

Introduction to Christianity

Almost two thousand years ago, a Jewish man named Jesus taught in the hills near the Sea of Galilee in Israel. His message fascinated people. He spoke of eternal peace and a relationship with God. His life echoed prophecies given seven hundred years before his birth. Crowds followed him everywhere. He healed, loved, cared, wept—he was human, but something was different.

The religious leaders of the day feared his message. Secular rulers mistook him for a rabble-rouser, a troublemaker. At the request of a large crowd, the Romans released a murderer and executed Jesus in his place.

His followers mourned his loss and feared they would soon face the same fate. Then a few weeks later, they were back out among the crowds, claiming Jesus was alive again, raised from the dead. They declared him the Messiah, or Christ, the King whom the Jewish prophets had promised. Some people believed this claim; others saw it as a dangerous distortion of Jewish faith.

Within a decade, the claim that Jesus was alive and was King of the world had spread to Syria and beyond. A group of believers in the Syrian town of Antioch were called Christians by their neighbors. It was probably meant as mockery, but the believers reveled in it. Christian—literally someone who is like Christ—was just what they wanted to be.

FRACTURED FAITH

Christians today are all too aware of how hard it is to live as Jesus would if he had their families, their schools, and their jobs. A while ago, a guy named Bobby told us how he lived three different lives, depending on where he was. He acted one way at work, another at home, and still another at church. "I feel fractured inside," he said. "There is Work Bobby, Out-at-the-Bars Bobby, and Church Bobby. I can't live with the inconsistency anymore!"

Bobby isn't alone. Many of us compartmentalize our lives into different areas: a church life, a school life, a work life, a family life — the list goes on. The result is an odd Christian life that never reflects what we say we believe. We desperately need a firm Christian worldview that applies to all of life. Once we know who we are and where we're going, we can stand strong no matter what storms come our way.

God

The Christian worldview starts with God. Everything else flows from him. Our view of God defines our identity as human beings, the problems we face in a world of suffering, our source of ultimate authority, and everything else. So who is God?

It would be impossible to describe the universe adequately in a few pages, so it's unthinkable to describe God, who is far more vast and complex. This will be only the barest sketch.

GOD IS LOVE

One of the writers of the Bible states that God is love.[1] That's nice, we think, and a dozen cheery songs come to mind. But the biblical writers don't sing pop songs. Love, to them, is the will to do good for another person—the decision and the action of doing whatever is good for the other, even at great cost to oneself. The Christian God's very essence is that of a Being with a will passionately committed to the good of the other.

In fact, God is relational in his essence. Christians believe God is eternally three Persons in one God. The Bible names these three Persons in various ways, but most commonly it describes God as the Father in an eternal and loving relationship with the Son, and the Holy Spirit overflows from that relationship. The Father is passionately committed to the good of the Son. The Son has the same passionate commitment to the Father. And both share that commitment to the Spirit, who in turn is wholly committed to whatever is good for them.

Christians call God's three-in-oneness the Trinity. It's hard to imagine a Being who is one God and yet is distinctly a Father, a Son, and a Spirit, but that's what the Christian Scriptures present. The love relationship lies at the heart of the Christian God.

GOD IS CREATOR

The Bible says the love overflowing from God was so rich that he decided to create a universe to love. As an Artist, he imagined and made the cosmos in all its intricate beauty, and he loved it. He was devoted to its good. He created at least one planet, Earth, with creatures whom he made capable of loving him back. (More on those creatures later.)

Breathe in, breathe out. Breathe in again. Now say out loud as you exhale, "Let there be light." Did anything happen? I didn't think so. Imagine the immense power God must have. He simply spoke, "Let there be . . ." and BOOM, it was! Incredible. God designed each tree and every animal. He thought up the idea of subatomic particles. Matter. Energy. Food. Sex. All his inventions.

The concept of God as the Creator is a nonnegotiable for a Christian worldview. When you read about other worldviews in the pages that follow, notice whether they do or don't think God created the universe. Having (or not having) a Creator affects our view of who we are. A biblical poet wrote:

> I can never escape from your spirit!
>> I can never get away from your presence!
> If I go up to heaven, you are there;
>> if I go down to the place of the dead, you are there. . . .
> You made all the delicate, inner parts of my body
>> and knit me together in my mother's womb.
> Thank you for making me so wonderfully complex![2]

GOD IS JUST AND MERCIFUL

God is committed to the good of his universe, and especially to the good of every living creature in it. In fact, the notion of goodness is rooted in God. Christians believe God's nature is the standard of what is good and not good. What God naturally does is good.

However, God has given some creatures, such as humans and angels, the freedom to choose whether or not to pursue each other's good. When a person is indifferent to another's good, or when she actively pursues another's harm, God calls that wrong. God hates wrongdoing. God relates to wrongdoers as a Judge. His passion for justice comes from his love, his passion for good. He doesn't enjoy punishing wrongdoers. He would rather that they change their ways. He is merciful and waits to forgive them. But his passion for the good of every creature demands that he treat stubborn wrongdoers with justice.

God's love is like the nuclear reaction that gives the sun its heat and light. It is blazing in beauty, breathtaking in power, a source of warmth and life for those who love its light, and a source of terror to those who prefer darkness.

GOD IS PERSONALLY INVOLVED IN HUMAN HISTORY

God placed the sun where it belongs in the solar system, at a safe distance from Earth so we don't become crispy critters. In a similar way, because we humans are habitually lacking in goodness, God maintains some distance from us for our own protection, so his blazing goodness doesn't destroy us. This incinerating aspect of God's goodness is called holiness. It's scary, but it's just his love looked at from another angle.

However, unlike the gods of some other religions, the Christian God doesn't confine himself to a safe distance. Instead, the Bible presents him as actively involved in human affairs from the beginning of history until today. In fact, human history is his plan for us worked out over time. He made the laws of physics and chemistry, and he rarely meddles with them, but at key moments he is free to do so without upsetting the balance of the universe, because he knows what he's doing. He made it, after all.

God is all-powerful and knows everything. Because he made time and exists outside time, he knows what will happen as well as what has happened.

He interacts personally with individual people and with groups. He talks to them. He wants them to talk to him. Personal relationship is essential to his nature. He is utterly beyond our comprehension, yet he wants to know and be known, to love and be loved. He doesn't need our love (he has plenty), and he has every right to demand our love, but instead, he asks for it. He doesn't grovel for it, though — he's still a blazing sun of pure goodness.

The ugliness of human history often depresses us. God, however, isn't discouraged. He is actively pursuing a plan for our planet's ultimate good. And even while there's a lot of ugliness on our planet, God overflows with joy. He has a whole beautiful universe to enjoy, and the Father and the Son and the Spirit have each other to enjoy. God is having a good time.

Humanity

I was about seven years old when I was introduced to modeling clay. The art teacher walked into my classroom and passed out lumps of the cool, slick clay. She told us to play with it for a while and squish it between our fingers. Most of the girls thought it was gross. Of course, the boys wanted more. What an amazing substance.

After we played with the clay for a while, the teacher stopped us. She told us to make something with it. We could create anything we wanted, but we only had fifteen minutes to transform our clay into something great.

With dreams of being the next Michelangelo, I went to work. I soon discovered that turning lumps of clay into works of art was hard. How did anyone ever make a sculpture? I tried and tried, but my attempts at making a person looked more and more like something my dog left in the yard. How frustrating!

When the teacher announced we had only five minutes left, I panicked. What was I going to show my parents? How would they know that I was the next great artist? So I did what any self-respecting seven-year-old would do. I copied what my friend was making.

Funny thing was, Spencer was making an ashtray. My parents didn't smoke. I don't even think his parents smoked. But short on time and lacking ideas, I made the exact same thing. Of course, my parents accepted my unique "bowl" lovingly, but I knew I had compromised my visions of grandeur and simply copied something.

THE BEAUTY OF CLAY

The Bible tells a story that likens God to an artist who bent and scooped up a lump of clay. As he worked the clay in his hands, he looked at all he had made: giraffes, parakeets, mushrooms, roses, even a platypus. He liked all of it. But something was missing. Despite the planet's splendor, he believed Earth lacked one element.

He pinched, tweaked, and twisted the clay in his hands. When he had finished, he set his new creation on the ground and breathed on it. It sprang to life and looked at God. God thought this new creature was good, but it was lonely. He put the clay creature into a deep sleep, took part of its side, and created something more beautiful than anything else he had made: a woman. He named the clay creature Adam and the woman Eve, and he declared them very good.

This marked the high point of God's creation, more spectacular than the stars. What made this lump of clay so special? God had shaped it in his own image. Not even the angels of heaven had that distinction. Man and woman were made in such a way that they could both know God intimately and reflect his glory in their day-to-day lives.

A DIFFERENT VISION OF HUMANITY

Many non-Christian worldviews view humanity differently. One of the more common views is that we evolved from other life-forms. If you follow this line of reasoning, you are nothing but a freak of chance. There is nothing special about you. You are simply another animal species that is flourishing for a brief period in the vast history of Earth. Cockroaches have been around longer and will outlast your species.

Other worldviews portray humans as slaves to the whims of the cosmos. Whether you call it chance, fate, or destiny, these worldviews think that forces control who you are and the choices you make.

By contrast, the Bible says Adam and Eve were God's special creation, made in his image. For example, the human drive to create art and technology, to garden and decorate, reflects the Creator's image. Our thirst for knowledge echoes his perfect wisdom. Our capacity to have intimate person-to-person relationships mirrors his relational nature. And our instinct to rule the world (often sadly abused) originally expressed our intended role on earth: to govern its plants and animals for the good of all, as God governs the universe for its good.

Every time you look in the mirror, you see the image of God. Every time you see another person, you behold God's reflection. This doesn't mean you're a god. Far from it. But you were meant to be God's personal representative among the species on earth. And every human person is of incalculable worth because she bears God's image.

The image of God in you also makes your salvation possible. Fallen angels can't be redeemed, nor can plants or animals know God personally. Only people.

The biblical tradition sees the image of God not just in the human soul, but also in the human body. If you think yours is too short or not shapely enough, God says you're mistaken. Some worldviews treat the body as the temporary prison of a soul that will move from body to body to body over many lifetimes. The Christian worldview sees humans as whole body-soul-spirit persons. What you do with your body, or someone else's body, matters because it carries God's image. And salvation involves the body as well as the soul.

THE TROUBLE WITH HUMANS

That's the good news: Humans were created as bearers of God's image. But we had one God-given quality that got us into trouble. God made us with the freedom to choose love or not love, good or not good. Love that isn't freely chosen isn't love—it's the response of a machine—so choice was a necessary part of our design. But in designing us this way, God foresaw the consequences.

The Bible tells how the first humans lived in a paradise, free to do anything they wanted, except one thing. They weren't told why that one thing was forbidden. The rule seemed arbitrary: Don't eat fruit from a particular tree. It seemed unreasonable. The fruit had many appealing qualities. It was a test. Would they trust that God was pursuing their good? Would they pursue what was good for him (their obedience)? Would they love and be loved? Or would they disregard love in pursuit of their own desires?

They stole the fruit. And into the human heart, which was formed in God's image, they carved a scar that every human after them has carried: "I want my way." "I want what I want when I want it." "I am the master of my fate, the ruler of my universe." The Bible calls it sin.

Sin makes it impossible for humans to have an intimate connection with God. God is pure love, and sin is loveless. Love pursues the other's good. Sin demands its own way, indifferent to the other's good. God's pure goodness would incinerate a sin-stained human, so God keeps his distance.

Sin doesn't erase God's image. It twists it. Our desires to create, to know, and to govern justly become compulsive drives to build empires, to tear things apart for their secrets, and to exploit the planet. Our longing for relationship leads us to use or be used. Sin clouds our minds so that we don't see and understand what's really going on. It deadens our emotions so that we crave stimulation. And it enslaves our will so that we sometimes find it impossible to choose someone else's good. Most of all, it kills our ability to connect with God. The Bible calls this spiritual deadness.

Salvation

The Bible describes God's centuries-long plan to rescue humans from spiritual deadness. This rescue plan is called salvation. God has to save us from the consequences of our self-centeredness and heal that "I want what I want" demand in our hearts so that it's both possible and safe for us to get close to him. Because even people who live fairly good lives still have that demand at their core, all of us need to be rescued from it.

God's rescue operation involved something that astounded even the angels. He came to earth as a human. The Bible says Jesus Christ was and is the eternal Son of God in human flesh. Fully God, fully human. During the thirtysomething years of his life, he demonstrated what God is like — what he loves and hates, how he deals with people. Jesus also demonstrated how a human acts when sin hasn't scarred the image of God in him. His life as a man gave even greater honor to the human body and human soul than they already had.

His death accomplished even more. When the Roman government executed Jesus on a cross, Jesus took on himself the accumulated guilt of all the evildoing that humans have done in the history of the world. He paid the price for it that God's justice required. In his love, God couldn't simply ignore wrongdoing. He had to do something about it.

In his death, Jesus defeated and killed the power self-absorbed sin has over us. Then he rose from the dead, because death had no more power over him. Because of his death and resurrection, it is now possible for us to be forgiven for our wrongdoing so we can be close to God. It is also now possible for us to cooperate with God in erasing from our minds and bodies the habits of sin. With his help we can, over time, break free of that "I want what I want when I want it" demand that drives so much of what we do.

This rescue from sin starts now and has an enormous effect on our lives here and now. It also affects what happens to us after we die, as we'll discuss below. God has done his part in this rescue operation, but we also have to do our part. We have to choose to accept his offer of forgiveness and reconciliation. We have to want to be freed from sin. We have to cooperate with his process of disentangling us from sin. Believing true things about God and Jesus can be a starting point, but being a Christian really means saying to God, and meaning it, that we love him and want him to be the center of our universe. We make this choice once, and then we make it again a hundred times every day. The hundred times a day gets easier, partly because when we make the decision the first time, God sends his Spirit to live inside us and influence our thinking and our will.

Christianity teaches that Jesus alone can rescue humans from sin. In the gospel of John, Jesus says, "I am the way, the truth, and the life. No one can come to the Father except through me."[1] No other religion, no other faith system, no other method of belief works. Other religions may have elements of truth or practical plans for living a life far better than utter self-centeredness. But other religions don't make a spiritually dead person alive. They don't reconnect a person with God. Only Jesus does that. Many people view this as an intolerant position, but this is what Christianity teaches. God offers this salvation to everyone. Each person has to respond for herself. From a Christian point of view, the most loving thing one friend can do for another is to introduce him to Jesus.

Authority

Our friend James grew up in a nice part of town and had just about everything he ever wanted. But James had a problem. He hated his dad telling him what to do all the time. His dad made him cut his hair a certain way. He couldn't wear some types of clothes. He had to be in bed by ten o'clock every night—even on weekends! But James had a plan. The day of his eighteenth birthday, James left his parents' house and marched down to the army recruiter's office.

About eight weeks after boot camp, James was on leave. He joked about the irony of the situation. He hated being told what to do, but he never even got to think for himself in the army. His commander told him what to do. The army set his schedule. They issued a uniform, and everyone had the same haircut. James had left something he thought was bad and exchanged it for the exact same thing.

The older we become, the more we realize that James' experience is no different from our own. Someone is always in a position of authority over us. Our boss, our teachers, our parents, God—you get the idea. There is no escaping authority.

Some of us resent this. We want to be the center of our own universe, answerable to no one. But the truth is, we all need help to get through life. We can't exhaustively investigate every issue with which life presents us, so we need to know who we can trust. Can we believe the scientists who say smoking will kill us? Or do we have to study biochemistry and read all the medical research on smoking for ourselves? In situations like these, authorities—sources of information that we can trust to a greater or lesser degree—help us rather than restrict us.

GOD

A Christian worldview asserts that God is the ultimate Authority. He created the universe, so he knows what he's talking about. Many of the worldviews we will examine in this book deny that any objective authority exists outside ourselves. If we eliminate God, humans are the final authority. But to believe in God is to acknowledge him as *the* Authority.

Adam and Eve faced exactly this decision. They decided to be their own authority and take God's place. Similarly, many worldviews say, "You are your own god! Do what you want. Don't let anyone tell you what to do."

THE BIBLE

While God is the ultimate Authority in our lives, he communicates that authority most importantly through the Bible. But what is the Bible, really? It was written by various men over centuries. It contains the Old Testament and the New Testament. The Old Testament begins with the account of the world's creation in the book of Genesis. It ends with prophecies and proclamations about the coming Messiah. The New Testament begins with the story of Jesus and ends with the return of Christ to earth at the end of days.

The Bible recounts how God related to many generations of men and women — individuals, groups, and nations. It shows us who he is by recording his words and describing him in action. One biblical writer, the apostle Paul, says this about the Bible:

All Scripture is *inspired* by God and is useful to *teach* us what is true and to *make us realize* what is wrong in our lives. It straightens us out and teaches us to do what is right. It is God's way of preparing us in every way, fully equipped for every good thing God wants us to do.[1]

Let's break this down a bit.

When Paul calls the Bible "inspired," the word literally means "God-breathed." Remember the account of creation? God breathed into Adam the breath of life. Similarly, the Bible has life and authority because God breathes life into its pages. Paul means that the Bible is completely trustworthy and true.

Some groups, such as Mormons and Muslims, believe God dictated their scriptures to a person who wrote them down. They believe that the personality and historical context of the human writer are irrelevant to understanding the text, because the writer was just the secretary. Christians don't view the Bible this way. They believe that God shaped the personalities of the biblical writers and placed them in cultural settings. The divine inspiration of the Bible doesn't erase the human element any more than Jesus' divinity lessens his humanity.

The Bible teaches us what is true and makes us realize what is wrong in our lives. Left to ourselves and our own devices, we will self-destruct. But Scripture teaches us how to live.

The author of the book of Hebrews tells us that "the Word of God is full of living power. It is sharper than the sharpest knife, cutting deep into our innermost thoughts and desires."[2] God knows our deepest thoughts and motivations. He uses the Bible to cut through the excuses, habits, or false ideas we cling to.

GOD'S PEOPLE

Since they have the Bible and a personal relationship with Christ, some Christians decide to live their Christian life in isolation. These "Lone Ranger" Christians believe they don't need anyone else's help to make it as a Christian. Such people have confused the Christian worldview with American individualism.

In the historic Christian worldview, relationships are central. We spend our lives learning how to do two things Jesus said were fundamental: love God and love others.[3] Love can't be learned or practiced alone. It's impossible. And to discourage Christians from trying to do it alone, God deliberately gives each individual only some of the gifts and abilities he or she needs to survive spiritually. Unless we team up, we wither.

Time

It hung high on the wall, the enemy of every kid in school. The big silver-rimmed clock never seemed to change. The smooth, sweeping motion of the second hand marked the passing of eternity as we waited desperately for the bell to ring for recess! The way most of us stared at the clock, you would have thought we were moving it forward simply by the force of our wills. The second the clock clicked over and the bell rang, we were free!

Life moved too slowly back then. It seemed like forever until we could get our driver's licenses or go to college or get married. Why did time pass so slowly? It was as if we were staring at that same clock from grade school, waiting.

Even though we can't wait to zip off into the future when we're kids, the older we become, the more we see time as the enemy. There never are enough hours in the day to do all that needs to be done. In our busyness, there never seems to be time to simply stop and rest. There is always a place to go, a goal to attain, another day at work, or another event to attend.

A CIRCLE OR A LINE

Some worldviews, such as Hinduism and Buddhism, see time as a circle. The seasons cycle endlessly from spring to summer to autumn to winter. Human life circles from birth to childhood to maturity to old age to death, and then to rebirth in another body through reincarnation. There is neither beginning nor end, and more importantly, there is no goal toward which time is heading. The only goal is to escape the endless cycle through enlightenment. We will talk more about this in the chapters on Hinduisim and Buddhism.

The Christian worldview acknowledges life's cyclical nature, but it sees time ultimately as a line with a beginning and an end. God exists outside time, and he created time when he created the universe. He created night and day to mark what we know as time. The sun rises and then sets, equaling one day. We sleep all night and are active during the day. This is the ebb and flow of life as we know it.

We don't know how humans would have experienced time if they hadn't rebelled against God. Before death, did time lack urgency? Genesis portrays God spending scheduled time each evening enjoying friendship with Adam and Eve. But after the rebellion, the human lifespan was limited. The clock was ticking. Even the earth and the universe itself will someday wear out.

God expected the rebellion, and the rest of human history is the story of his plan to rescue us. The plan has played out, and continues to play out, over time. History is going somewhere. God chose a man to be the father of a nation, Israel. He shaped that nation over centuries. They spent generations waiting for him to send the Messiah he promised. The Messiah was born on a particular day, lived, and was sentenced to death on another day.

As Jesus hung on the cross, it was as if time stood still. What would happen? The Son of God was bleeding, dying.

Jesus' dead body occupied a tomb for roughly nine hours on a Friday and all of a Saturday. Early on Sunday, God raised him from the dead.

Jesus spent forty days training his followers to spread the word about what he'd done. Then he left our physical world and sent in his place the Spirit of God. Since then, his followers have been carrying out his work in the world and waiting—for centuries—for him to return to bring human history as we know it to a glorious close. Christians look forward to that day like kids counting the days until summer vacation. But because we don't know that date, we try to stay focused on whatever God has given us to do today.

I'M GONNA LIVE FOREVER

Step right up, ladies and gentlemen! How would you like to live forever? Today and today only, we are offering a special on eternal life!

Christians believe that all humans will exist in some form eternally. The Bible offers glimpses of this destiny in references to heaven, hell, a new heaven, and a new earth. The biblical writers speak of heaven as a feast, a wedding, a glorious city. Fundamentally, there is only one place to go beyond death: into the blazing light of the sun, the presence of God. For those who love the light, this will be the unveiling of the beauty they have longed for all their lives. Those who love darkness will view it differently. Dorothy Sayers, translator of Dante's *Divine Comedy*, wrote that "the fire of Hell is simply the light of God as experienced by those who reject it; to those, that is, who hold fast to their darling illusion of sin, the burning reality of holiness is a thing unbearable."[1]

Also, because humans are body-soul-spirit, our ultimate destiny isn't as immortal disembodied souls. Those who embrace the light will have physical bodies, just as Jesus has a body—not a resuscitated corpse, but a body that is dramatically different yet recognizably a body. This is called resurrection, not to be confused with reincarnation, which involves a return to this world in one body after another.

The Bible indicates that resurrected people will retain their uniqueness as persons with personalities. In fact, those who love the light will become more uniquely the person each of them was meant to be, while those who love darkness will find their souls shriveling into a boring sameness.

Christians look forward to life beyond death with eager expectation. But there's a lot to do with the time we have now. The image of God in us needs to be strengthened and used. Compulsive self-centeredness needs to be overcome. All Christians share in God's work in the world: seeking the good of every person and the whole planet.

Jesus

The sun washed over the valley where Jesus and his friends were walking. They laughed and talked about what they had experienced over the past few weeks. Could anyone forget how Jesus fed a crowd with just a few loaves of bread? He had even healed a blind man by spitting in the dirt and applying the mud to his eyes. Everybody in the country knew Jesus was no ordinary man.

As they walked, he asked his followers what the people were saying about him. "A great prophet," answered one. Another quoted the rumor that Jesus was the wonder-working prophet Elijah returned to earth. Jesus stopped. His friends gathered closely. "But who do *you* say I am?" he asked.

If we are going to understand the Christian worldview, we must know who Jesus Christ is and why he came.

TEACHER

First (but not last), he was a great teacher. Part of his mission was to teach how God wanted his people to live. His teachings speak for themselves, and many other worldviews recognize their greatness. In fact, some non-Christians who know great teaching when they see it, such as Gandhi, have wondered why so few Christians seem to live according to these obviously brilliant ideas.

GOD AND MAN

Yet he was far more than a teacher. He was God. The Son of God, the perfect self-expression of God, took on the flesh and blood of a man. He experienced the best and the worst of human life — friendship and betrayal, weddings and funerals, hunger, exhaustion, daily hardships, and immense suffering.

He was a manual laborer in a backwater region of an underdeveloped country. He deliberately chose a role that would make him a servant rather than a man of wealth and power. And he endured it all without sinning. He never lost his focus on his Father's good and our good, no matter what it cost him.

The central theme of his teaching was the kingdom of God. Jesus came as King of the realm in which God's will is done. Most of the universe belongs to that realm, as the stars, planets, and angels do what God made them to do, either by nature or by choice. The human race is in rebellion against God's kingdom, and Jesus came to invite us to quit the rebellion and join his side. He demonstrated the signs of God's kingdom: freeing people from disease, evil, and even death.

SAVIOR

Freeing people from evil and death was the ultimate reason why he came. After training his followers in the ways of his kingdom, he let the authorities subject him to the most humiliating death known at that time: crucifixion. He died in our place.

Ever since Adam and Eve, death had been the consequence of rebellion against God. Because life came from God, rejecting God meant choosing death. And because God is holy, justice demanded that the harm done by a wrongdoer couldn't simply be wished away. It had to be paid for. But because God is love, he decided to pay for it himself. On the cross, Jesus the Son of God took upon himself the justly deserved punishment for all the loveless acts of all the men and women who ever lived. He suffered the utter separation from the Father that sin causes. He endured it all the way to death. And in doing so, he freed those who take him as their King from having to pay the ultimate penalty. In his death he fulfilled the requirements of

God's love—both justice against evil and mercy toward evildoers in a single act. In this act, he reconciled rebellious humans to their true Lord.

RISEN LORD

Jesus came to live in mortal flesh, to teach, to heal, to die, and finally to rise from the dead. His resurrection proves that death has no power over his followers. We may die, but we too will rise. We don't have to fear getting old, because someday we will have ageless bodies. We don't have to fear parting from our loved ones who also love him, because we'll meet them again. We don't have to worry that we don't have enough time in this life to get done everything important, because we have eternity ahead of us. We don't have to grab for all the pleasure and possessions this life can offer, because this life isn't all there is. Jesus is alive now with the Father, still bearing his resurrected human body. And someday we'll have bodies like his.

Some of the implications of this view of Jesus are:

1. *God is near.* Some religions think of God as distant and detached from human affairs. But the God of the Bible sent his own Son to die for humans. He cares and is here with us now.

2. *We can know God.* Jesus told his followers, "Anyone who has seen me has seen the Father."[1] To know Jesus is to know and experience God.

3. *Jesus deserves our worship.* We can pray to him and he hears us, just like the Father. Paul tells us that one day everyone will bow at the name of Jesus.[2]

4. *Jesus knows what we're going through.* As a man, Jesus faced the same temptations each of us faces, but he never gave in. He stands today before the throne of the Father interceding for us. Because he knows by experience everything we face, he knows what we need and when we need it.[3]

5. *Jesus is our example.* Jesus endured every temptation we endure, yet he didn't sin. We can read about and imitate the things he did to stay focused on what was right. Also, if we actively rely on the Spirit who lives in us, we can endure under any trial. When we fail, Jesus offers forgiveness and another chance. With that help, we can press on through any challenge in life.

2

Theism—Worldviews Centered on God(s)

Introduction to Theism
Hinduism
Buddhism
Islam

Though we may not experience him (or her) directly, God (however you choose to define him or her) is involved in the cosmos somehow.

Introduction to Theism

For many people, the idea of something or someone beyond this life dominates their worldview. This something is often understood as a god—a being that is not human but exercises some control over human beings or human experiences. Sometimes personal, sometimes unknowable, these gods fulfill a human desire to know and experience the world beyond the reality we can experience through our five senses. In this section we'll discuss the major theistic worldviews. Before we dive into the formal belief systems, let's start by looking at a few of the unique landmarks and terms we will encounter while exploring the vistas of theism.

The first thing we need to define is the word **theism*** (words like this in bold font with an asterisk are defined in the glossary at the end of each chapter). Theism is the belief that a god or a supreme being is involved in the world we observe around us. Most people in the world understand the universe through the lens of theism. For example, Christians and Jews are theists. Both believe God created and sustains the universe. Christianity stands apart with its belief that God establishes a direct relationship with humanity through the person and work of Jesus Christ.

While Judaism and Christianity believe in a similar concept of God, other theistic worldviews work differently. Hinduism suggests there are multiple gods that are worthy of worship, while Buddhism stresses the unifying power of what is called the Absolute. Other worldviews, such as naturalism, argue that theism is the wrong way to think about the world and stand in opposition to theistic understandings of creation.

Now that we know a bit of the lay of the land, let's explore some of these ideas about theism.

MONOTHEISM

Judaism, Islam, and Christianity all believe there is one God. This one God created the universe and everything that exists. Belief in only one God is called **monotheism***. Even though these three religions share a belief in monotheism, the similarity ends there. They have significantly different religious systems and understandings about who God is. Christianity has much in common with the Jewish concept of God. Both recognize the Old Testament as the Word of God. However, the person of Christ divides Jews and Christians. Jews do not recognize Jesus as the Messiah, nor do they accept the Trinitarian understanding of God.

Muslims are also monotheistic. They believe that Allah is the one god of the universe. According to the Koran, Allah removes himself from involvement with humans on a daily basis. This stands in sharp contrast to the way the Bible describes God's involvement in the lives of his followers. We will discuss more of the differences between Islam and Christianity a bit later.

POLYTHEISM

Not all theistic religions are monotheistic, however. In fact, many religions believe in multiple beings, spirits, or gods to whom honor is due. Belief in more than one god is called **polytheism***. At the time of Jesus, most cultures were polytheistic. Monotheists like the Jews were rare and viewed with suspicion. Today, the two dominant polytheistic worldviews are Hinduism and Buddhism. You can find chapters on each of these worldviews in this section. Some of the ideas put forward by polytheists will stress a unifying principle in the universe that combines many of the best concepts of monotheism into the practice of polytheism. You will hear echoes of this in the Hindu idea of Brahman and the Buddhist concept of the Absolute.

PANTHEISM

Pantheism* takes the concept of theism to a different level by stressing that everything is God. The rocks, trees, animals, and even humans are all expressions of God. Pantheists say this belief puts a positive spin on the human condition. Humans aren't sinners or unenlightened or victims of fate. We are God. Many ancient religions were pantheistic, and the idea appeals to many people today who follow New Age religions, neo-paganism (which is more pantheistic than polytheistic), or Wicca.

Gene Roddenberry, creator of the famous *Star Trek* series, abandoned Christianity for a pantheistic worldview. Despite being raised in a Christian environment, Roddenberry and his wife thought they found a better system that emphasized the divinity within everyone and everything.

> My second wife Majel Lee and I were both raised Protestant but well before ever meeting both left the Protestant Church in favor of non-sectarian beliefs which included respect for all other religions, but emphasizing the concept of God as too great and too encompassing to be explained and appreciated by any single system of belief. Upon meeting we found that both believed in the brotherhood of all life forms, human and otherwise.[1]

Pantheism often appeals to radical environmentalists who want to hold on to a belief in the divine. If everything in nature is somehow equal to or is God, then caring for nature is the most important thing we can do. For some pantheists, the concept of calling our planet "Mother Earth" reflects this connection between the divinity of all living beings.

Of course, not all environmentalists are pantheists, and caring for our planet should be important to everyone, even Christians. There are basic differences in the approach, however. While Christianity would talk about environmentalism as part of humanity's stewardship of God's creation, pantheism stresses the equality of all beings. In the pantheistic mindset, a plant is just as divine a being as a person. Holding to this pantheistic idea, Henry David Thoreau argued that lumberjacks cutting down trees were actually murdering them and should be punished.[2]

PANENTHEISM

No, this isn't a repeat of the previous section. The addition of the letters "en" in the middle of the word change the meaning. **Panentheism*** is the belief that everything in the world — rocks, trees, animals, humans — is *in* God, rather than *is* God. You might stop me here because your brain is hurting. What is the basic difference? Why even differentiate between the two? To be honest, some people don't. But because some professors in your religion classes may draw a distinction between the two, we've included it here.

To understand the difference that little "en" makes, let's visit the Gap. You enter the store and find several sweaters you like. You decide to try some on. In the dressing room, you pull the sweater over your head to see how it fits. Now stop. Imagine that sweater as God. You are "in" the sweater. It covers you, but it is not the same as you. This is what panentheists believe. Humans and all of nature are simply "in" God.

So what's wrong with that idea for the Christian? Isn't that what the Bible teaches us? Hold up there. There is a big differ-ence. Most panentheists construct their idea of God as a simple force that pervades the universe, covering and even animating just about everything. A good example might be the *Star Wars* concept of the "Force." In the *Star Wars* series, the Force could be good and it could be bad, but it was always there in a mystical, almost creepy way.

Similarly, panentheism paints the image that everything is in God and some of God's power or properties are transferred to it because God or a God-force animates everything. Christianity teaches that God is a Being, a Person who thinks and loves. He is separate from creation because he made it. When the apostle Paul says that "in him we live and move and have our being,"[3] Paul doesn't mean God is simply the covering or connection by which everything exists. Creation is not "in" him in that sense. He is a being all to himself and is not to be depersonalized or equated with anything that he made. At the same time, Christianity asserts God is present. Even though he is different from us, he still participates with us in life.

ATHEISM

Atheism* is the belief that there is no God at all. Atheists rely on science to explain all of nature. They believe truth exists not in religion, but in humans themselves. Some atheists argue religion is a crutch to help emotionally challenged people get through life. If people used logic and reason to think through life's issues, they would abandon any idea of God. While most atheists tolerate other people's religious convictions, some seem to stop at nothing until they convince everyone that God doesn't exist.

You will probably encounter atheism mostly during your years at university or college. Plenty of professors have abandoned the idea of God and dismissed religion as bogus. It may even surprise some of your professors that you believe in God at all. We don't have time to deal exhaustively with the evidences for creation and God in this book, but you need to be prepared for encounters with those who will work hard to convince you that God doesn't exist. They'll argue that your beliefs are invalid. We'll talk more about this system of thought when we discuss secular humanism.

AGNOSTICISM

Okay, so this word doesn't have the word "theism" as part of its makeup, but it fits into our discussion here. **Agnosticism*** says that if there is a God, it is impossible for us as humans to know or experience such a Being. Agnostics are often people who have left the religion they grew up in but can't fully deny that God exists. Instead, they default to the position that God can't be known. This appeals to many people. It allows them to worship at church or synagogue and continue traditions they grew up with or enjoy, without putting any faith into their religion. It's simply a practice of tradition.

Some of America's founding fathers took this line. They followed a belief system called **deism***. They believed that God created the universe, set it in motion, and then left it alone. God still existed out there somewhere, but he didn't make himself known in a way that humans could experience. Deists substituted science and other human ideas for God's revelation. In their minds, the Bible couldn't be trusted, because it was simply a human invention. However, they did acknowledge that it contained good ideas to live by. They argued that if the Creator God did exist, why would he care about the world anyway?

Deism eventually died out. Today's agnostics look at the universe differently. Like atheists, they demand scientific evidence that God exists or rational proof that he involves himself in human affairs. They don't see the Bible as offering anything necessary to human life. Instead, by stressing that people can't know God at all, they border on atheism for all practical purposes and often voice their opposition to religious groups.

MOVING ON . . .

Now that you have some idea about the different types of theism, we'll explore the theistic worldviews of some major religions. The remaining chapters in this section contain information about theistic philosophies. Some border on pantheism or panentheism, but none are atheistic or agnostic. We will wait for later sections to talk more about those reactions to theism. As we go on, please remember that the overviews of these religious worldviews are simply that—overviews. Volumes could be written about each worldview and its application of theory and religion. Some religions, such as Hinduism, are very complex. We'll try to get a handle on the key elements of each worldview so that you're able to recognize it when you encounter it.

THEISM GLOSSARY

Agnosticism — The belief that if there is a God, there is no way we humans could know or experience such a Being.

Atheism — The belief that there is no God.

Deism — A deviation from Christianity in the seventeenth and eighteenth centuries that argued God could not be intimately known. God simply created the world and then left it to work on its own.

Monotheism — The belief that there is only one God in the universe. Often this God is viewed as both the Creator and Sustainer of the universe.

Panentheism — The belief that everything is in God. The God-force animates the cosmos. Panentheists usually think of God as a presence or a force instead of a person or being.

Pantheism — The belief that everything is God. All of nature and all elements of the cosmos are, in fact, God.

Polytheism — The belief that there are multiple gods or divine beings in the cosmos that affect humans in a variety of ways.

Theism — The belief that a god or being is involved in the world we see and experience around us.

Hinduism

George Harrison had it made. As a guitarist for the Beatles, he had everything he wanted, yet he felt hollow inside. In his twenties, he grew tired of material success and started looking for God. He had been exposed to Christianity as a child and didn't think he would find answers there. On a trip to India, he was impressed with its gurus and religious leaders. After several years of study, Harrison embraced Hinduism. His song "My Sweet Lord," in which he sang the "Hare Krishna" mantra in the background vocals, made it to the top ten on the pop charts in 1969. Until his death in 2001, he followed the teachings of Hinduism in his quest to find the answers his soul searched for.

Perhaps it was the Beatles or the spirit of the sixties, but Hinduism has made major inroads since then all across America. With a shrinking global economy, many people working in finance, the sciences, education, and information technology increasingly find Hindus in their sphere of acquaintances. Even popular TV shows like *The Simpsons* feature Hindu characters as part of their regular cast.

Of all the religions that provide a foundation for a worldview, few could be harder to describe than Hinduism. As one of the oldest religions in the world, its traditions, ideas, and philosophies filter into many other worldviews, including Buddhism and the New Age movement. Hindus don't worship a central figure. They don't have a Jesus or a Muhammad or any single founder upon whose teaching the religion rests. Instead, the many gurus, sages, and philosophers in the Hindu system each teach a unique form of the religion. This makes it harder to classify, but we can start at its roots.

DHARMA, KARMA, AND MOKSHA

Most practitioners of Hinduism live in India. Even the terms *Hindu* and *India* derive from the same Sanskrit word for the Indus River. Most Hindus believe you must be born a Hindu to truly be a Hindu. Add to this the idea that once you are a Hindu, you can never be anything but a Hindu, and you have a sizable segment of the world population that practices some element of this religion. How many? More than 600 million in India itself and some 20–30 million in other parts of the world.[1] In round numbers, this is one out of ten people on the planet.

To grasp the basics of the Hindu system, you need to understand three concepts. The first is **dharma***. This term can be translated as "law," but the idea of dharma expands beyond human rules or regulations. It is understood to be the absolute law of the cosmos. Everything in the universe operates in relation to dharma—the rotation of the planets, the laws of gravity, and even human morality. Hindus view dharma as the one constant element in life. Associated with the Hindu god **Brahman***, dharma is the eternal expression of the timeless creator.

Dharma is also a person's duty. A person should live according to the eternal dharma that most branches of Hinduism teach. To follow dharma, a person needs to be rightly devoted to the gods and follow the moral and ethical teaching of the sages and philosophers who have gone before. By doing this, a Hindu's belief and practice of dharma reflects the eternal dharma of the universe.

The second foundational Hindu concept is **karma***. It is the rule of life for every living being. Karma reflects the cause-and-effect relationship of the universe. In the Hindu understanding of karma, a person's actions or deeds always have consequences.

If I leave my car in neutral, it will roll down a hill. In the same way, for a Hindu, if he chooses to do something immoral, he generates bad karma. Then, if he chooses to do something noble, the bad karma dissolves.

The idea of karma leaves no room for grace or forgiveness. There is no Being out there who can or will forgive. Thus, a person must always pay for every wrong action he commits. No one else can do this for him. Only the person who committed the deed can undo the problem. Because of this, Hindus believe religion helps people do more and more good things until the debt of karma is completely dissolved.

Karma must be understood in the vast cycle of life and reincarnation. *Incarnation* means to have a body, so *reincarnation* thus means to have a new body over and over again. Hindus believe it often takes multiple lives to get rid of bad karma generated in earlier lives. Because the Hindu system is built on a concept of cycles of life, a person may be reincarnated as a thing or an animal if his karma is bad enough. As the debt of karma is slowly erased over multiple incarnations, a Hindu rises to higher and higher levels of awareness. The ultimate goal is to escape the repetition of these life cycles.

Escape from the karmic cycle is the third main concept of Hinduism: **moksha***. If a Hindu performs enough good deeds to erase all karma, then a rebirth will not happen. Instead, she will finally be liberated. The liberation from the cycle of reincarnation is also referred to as **nirvana***. In nirvana, a person becomes one with the cosmos. If a person can actually escape the cycle of karma, a new unification with the universe happens. In other words, a person's soul unifies with what Hindus call "ultimate reality." This is sometimes difficult for people to grasp. Nirvana is not a physical place like heaven. Instead, it is ceasing to exist altogether. Some describe it as a drop of water returning to the ocean. When the droplet hits the water, any difference between the raindrop and the ocean disappears. They are one, and the drop ceases to be.

BORN TO A CASTE

When many people living in the West think about Hinduism or India, two images come to mind: cows in the street and the **caste system***. We'll deal with the cows later, but what about the caste system? Why does it exist at all? Modern India outlawed the caste system, but its practice has a long history and still deeply affects Hindu society.

Originally, the caste system served to keep portions of society separated from one another. Each caste performed specific duties to make society work smoothly. People were born into a specific caste and couldn't change it. Marriage outside of their caste was forbidden. If they chose to violate the caste system, they literally became an *outcaste*, an "untouchable."

There were four levels to the caste system. The **Brahmins*** occupied the highest caste and originally served as priests for the people. The second caste contained the warriors. Called **Kshatriyas***, they defended the law and upheld justice. Many in this second level filled the nobility and high-ranking military offices.

Below them were the **Vaishyas***. These people served as farmers or merchants. Their karma demanded they produce the goods and services that others consumed. This group was larger than the first two, but the largest segment of the populace fell into the fourth caste, the **Sudras***.

The Sudras served all the caste levels above them. They weren't slaves, but the caste system dictated it was their karmic duty to attend to the needs of the Brahmins, Kshatriyas, and Vaishyas. Usually the Sudras were blocked from education and lived underappreciated lives. They were better off than the outcastes, however. Without even a place on the scale, the outcastes had no rights. As outcastes, others viewed them as karmic lepers. The other castes banned the outcastes from the temples. Even touching an outcaste would make a caste member unclean.

The caste rules are carefully explained in a book called the **Bhagavad Gita***. The distinctions between the castes are designed so that each person can be perfected according to his or her karma. No one can change castes in this life, but if she works hard and follows the teachings of Hindu scriptures, she might be reincarnated in a higher caste in the next life. The higher she moves in the caste system through the cycles of reincarnation, the closer she gets to moksha.

WHAT'S UP WITH THE COWS?

In movies of India, you may notice a lot of cows walking around. To many people in the West, this is confusing. In a country where many people are starving, why don't they eat the cattle that roam free?

Hindus in India refuse to eat the free-roaming cows. Because the animal selflessly gives of itself to others, Hindus revere the cow as sacred. During certain parts of the year, the cows receive the same honor as other gods. The people anoint cows with expensive oils and place garlands around the animals' necks. Farmers who release a cow to wander the streets receive social honor and are thought to remove bad karma. The milk and other by-products, like the dung, are free to whoever needs them. For example, in the more economically depressed areas of the country, the dung is used as medicine, a disinfectant, fuel for fires, and countless other uses.

Gandhi called this practice "cow protection." He tried to explain it to a Western audience by stating, "She is the mother to millions of Indian mankind. The cow is a poem of pity. Protection of the cow means protection for the whole dumb creation of God."[2] While Hindus value the lives of all creatures, protection of a giving animal reflects a desire to protect all of creation.

Now that we have answered a few basic questions about Hinduism, let's turn to the six main points of interest that we examine at every scenic overlook.

WORLDVIEW SIGNPOSTS

God

According to one count of all the gods in the Hindu pantheon, there are more than 3.3 million gods to be worshiped.[3] Some are male, others female. Some are represented with heads of elephants, monkeys, cows, or other animals. At the same time, most Hindus believe in what they call the Absolute—a cosmic force that created and brings unity to the universe. Nirvana is joining with this force and ceasing to exist as a separate and unique person.

Most Hindus in India hold to a belief called **polytheism***. They worship many gods but usually elevate one above all others. This polytheistic concept is often referred to as **henotheism***. Henotheism allows for the elevation of one god while recognizing that other deities exist. While Hindus affirm that there is only one unifying principle worshiped as the Absolute, it is up to each individual Hindu to decide which god will provide the most direct path to moksha. In their day-to-day worship, many Hindus honor one specific god throughout the day. Some teachers of Hinduism have even claimed Buddha and Jesus.

One interesting aspect of Hindu worship is the way the gods are depicted. You may have seen the many-armed, somewhat human-looking statues and wondered what they mean. For Hindus, these representations contain reminders of the powers each god possesses and why he or she should be worshiped. Let's discuss some of these gods, and we'll try to explain why they are depicted as they are.

Brahman. Brahman is the unidentifiable force of the cosmos and is inaccessible to human thought. Since Brahman (do not confuse this with the Brahmins, the highest caste in Hinduism) cannot be contained in human thought, Hindus avoid worshiping him altogether. Instead, they worship the many aspects of Brahman, some of which date back more than a thousand years before Christ.

One aspect of Brahman is the god Indra, who represents light and victory. He is often represented with a thunderbolt. In Hindu mythology, Indra overcame the powers of darkness with this thunderbolt and allows the sun to rise every day.

Another aspect is Agni, the god of fire. In ancient times, Hindus offered sacrifices to the gods on altars with fire. Agni was understood as the one who took the offerings up to the Absolute.

There are several other aspects of Brahman, but it would take too long to list them all. For many Hindus, all the gods represented in the Hindu pantheon are simply aspects of Brahman or the Absolute. Today, the most popular gods worshiped by Hindus are understood as a trinity of sorts. Called the **Trimurti***, it is comprised of **Brahma***, **Vishnu***, and **Shiva***. These gods are thought to be indistinguishable from one another, while at the same time revealing unique aspects of the Absolute.

Brahma. Brahma is thought of as the creator god who brought Earth into existence. Don't confuse him with Brahman, because he isn't the Absolute, just an expression of the Trimurti. Depicted as having four faces that reflect the directions north, south, east, and west, he carries the Hindu scriptures in his hands. Those following Brahma are much fewer in number than those who worship Vishnu or Shiva. However, most temples still contain an area devoted to a statue of Brahma.

Vishnu. The protector of divine law, Vishnu has a large following. According to legend, any time divine law is severely challenged, Vishnu appears as an **avatar***. When we IM or discuss things on the Web, we often use avatars as images that represent who we are or how we're feeling to others on the Web. This is an idea taken directly from Hinduism. An avatar of Vishnu is an expression of who he is. At certain times in history when the eternal law was challenged, Vishnu appeared as an avatar to help reinstate the law of the Absolute. Hindus believe in ten avatars of Vishnu. Nine have already appeared, and one named Kalki will appear in the future. Kalki will usher in the final age of peace and unity according to Hindu tradition.

A well-known avatar of Vishnu is Krishna. Krishna is the focus of the Bhagavad Gita, one of the more popular scripture texts in Hinduism. Most Hindu artists paint Krishna with dark blue skin. The skin color demonstrates that he identifies with the darker-skinned "common" people. Those worshiping Krishna believe he cares for humans and steps in to aid them whenever there is danger.

Shiva. Harder to characterize than Vishnu or Brahma, Shiva takes many forms in the Hindu belief system. Hindus believe Shiva blesses and destroys at the same time. How can a god bless and destroy? One guru described it like an old building that must be torn down to make way for new housing in an area. There is destruction, but the blessing that comes from a new home for many is greater. Artists portray Shiva with a crescent moon in his hair, the symbol of the seasons, and a third eye on his forehead.

Shiva has been given many names by gurus and sages through the years, but all contain the basic ideas represented in blessing and destroying. One popular image of Shiva is as Nataraja, the Lord of the Dance. This image portrays Shiva standing on one foot with the other raised high. There are often four arms coming from Shiva's shoulders, symbolizing the way he manages creation, preserves, destroys, and liberates.

Other gods. Hindus worship other gods that reflect the forces of nature or give different blessings. For example, **Ganesha***, the son of Shiva, is shown as a human with an elephant's head. People worship Ganesha today as a god of good fortune who helps people escape difficulty.

Hindus worship the god they think will help them attain moksha as soon as possible. Because they have more than three million gods to choose from, Hinduism has vast variety in practices.

Humanity

In the Hindu system of thought, humanity is trapped in the repetitive cycle of rebirth. Hindus believe every person has a piece of the Absolute dwelling inside of him or her. This piece of the Absolute longs for liberation and wants to return to the Absolute. By offering sacrifices and right worship to the gods, each person comes closer to reaching moksha and final liberation. Because of the proliferation of gods, it is up to the human to read the Hindu scriptures and decide which path or which god is best to follow to eventually gain liberation.

Salvation

Hindus can travel one of three main paths for the removal of bad karma. The first is the way of works. In this system, people find salvation through living rightly and worshiping the gods. If they do everything correctly, Hindus believe they will be reincarnated in ever-higher levels until they attain moksha. In the caste system, this means working hard to do the tasks of your caste with the hopes of moving to a higher caste in the next life.

This system of reward corresponds to the ideas of karma. Salvation or liberation will happen after all karma dissolves. However many lives this takes, the path will not be shortened. Through doing good works, you slowly work off your debt of karma and attain moksha.

The second path is the way of knowledge. Hindus choosing this path to salvation believe that the root of the human problem is mental error. They can attain liberation through right thinking that gives victory over evil thoughts. Many gurus meditate to clear the mind and focus on the Absolute. To help attain the intense focus needed to purify the mind, they invented the system of yoga.

The third path strives for liberation through devotion. Those following this path believe that through devotion to specific deities, they will understand the way to final liberation. The deity enlightens the Hindu so he can trust the devotional path to remove him from the cycle of death and rebirth.

No matter which path is chosen, salvation for the Hindu involves escaping from the cycle of reincarnation and becoming one with the Absolute. In other words, a Hindu longs to be free from having a body and from being an individual person. By contrast, a Christian hopes to be resurrected with a body as a unique person in loving relationship with God.

Authority

Hindus base their religion on several scriptures, which fall into basic divisions. The **Shruti*** are scriptures to be heard, and the **Smriti*** are scriptures to be remembered. The Shruti consist of the four Vedas, which the gods gave to aid humanity. Most of the contents of the Vedas are hymns to gods during times of sacrifice. The Smriti texts are legends and lore about the gods along with legal and ethical texts that don't carry the same weight as the divinely inspired Shruti. One of these Smriti texts is the Bhagavad Gita that we have referenced a few times.

Although inspired texts are available, the individual still chooses how to remove his karma. Hindu religious leaders teach a variety of methods. Inherent in Hinduism, then, is tolerance for all branches of Hinduism, because they all strive for the same goal. This attitude boils over into tolerance for other religions as well. Many Hindus believe that all religions seek the same things and therefore must be seeking the same god. Although all religions do *not* seek the same god, and their goals may be very different from moksha or nirvana, many religions today nevertheless borrow the Hindu concept of tolerance.

Time

Because the Absolute is eternal and everyone contains a piece of the Absolute inside of them, Hindus believe we are eternal as well. Final liberation occurs when the soul joins the Absolute. Heaven as a physical or spiritual place doesn't exist. Instead, the state of nirvana is the extinguishing of karma in a person's life. After all karma is removed, the person trapped in the cycle of reincarnation returns to the Absolute to become one with it. Hinduism teaches that all souls long to achieve that final liberation in which the individual soul ceases to exist as unique and separate.

Jesus

Most Hindus accept that Jesus existed. He is usually viewed as a great guru who taught great things about the Absolute. Hindus often claim Jesus taught things that are compatible with the general teachings of Hinduism. Some traditions view Jesus as an avatar of Vishnu. Other gurus believe Jesus simply taught another way to reach the Absolute. At best, most Hindus would agree that if a person lived a moral Christian life, he could hope to be reincarnated as a Hindu and be one step closer to moksha.

HINDUISM AND CHRISTIANITY

Although the Hindu idea that all religions are aiming at the same thing has heavily influenced our culture, it's important at this point to clarify the ways Hindus and Christians view the world differently. Hindus believe that the dharma, or law, taught by their religion is the one eternal law. Christians believe the way of life Jesus taught is the right way to live. While there are many overlaps, there are also essential differences.

First, the Hindu Absolute is an impersonal cosmic force, uninvolved in human affairs. The Christian God is a Person who involves himself directly in human affairs. Christians would say that Jesus is not one of many avatars of the god Vishnu, but the only incarnation of the one God. Also, the Bible insists that no other gods but God exist. Therefore, henotheism (believing many gods exist while choosing one to worship) is not an option for people who follow the Bible.

Christians and Hindus also disagree about the ultimate goal of religion. Hindus aim at ceasing to be reborn with a body, ceasing to exist as unique persons, and becoming one with the Absolute. Christians aim at bodily resurrection for eternal life as unique persons in loving relationship with God.

Hindus seek to attain their goal by right living, right worship of the gods, or right knowledge. All of these are ways of erasing the karma of wrong thoughts and actions. Christians agree that wrong thoughts and actions are central to the human problem, but Christians don't think humans are capable of enough right knowledge, worship, and living to erase this wrong through their own efforts. Christians think people need to be extended grace and forgiven. Only a personal God can forgive. There is no Hindu counterpart to the forgiveness that Christians believe Jesus' death and resurrection attained. Christians believe a person has to put aside other gods and follow Jesus in order to receive that forgiveness.

Christians believe that right knowledge, worship, and living are important ways of responding to what God has done for them through Jesus. What constitutes "right" in these areas can be learned from the Bible and differs in important ways from the right knowledge, worship, and living taught by Hindus. For Christians, a relationship of love has to lie at the root of any knowledge, worship, or act to make it right in God's eyes.

To a Hindu, the best a Christian or Buddhist can hope for is to spend his life doing good, and thereby earn the good karma needed to be reincarnated as a Hindu. From there, the reincarnated person might eventually realize moksha.

As we leave this scenic overlook and head back onto the road of life, remember the concepts you learned here. You will encounter them again as we pull off the road at our next vista, Buddhism.

HINDUISM GLOSSARY

Avatar—Form that a god may take during specific moments in time. Those that have occurred in the past are seen as further expressions of the character of the god. These incarnations of the god aid in the worshiper's devotion.

Bhagavad Gita—A book of Hindu philosophy. When translated, the title actually means "Song of God." Most of the content is poetic in form and reveals a dialogue between Hindu gods.

Brahma—The creator god and part of the Trimurti. He is depicted with four faces representing the four directions: north, south, east, and west.

Brahman—The Absolute. The cosmic force of the universe that cannot be understood by humans.

Brahmins—The highest caste in the Hindu caste system. Brahmins were originally viewed as priests. Today, people who still identify with this caste serve as lawyers, businesspeople, politicians, and other high positions.

Caste System—Four ancient and distinct divisions in society imposed by the Hindu system. Outlawed during the twentieth century in India, it still carries weight in some segments of society. People are born into a caste. One cannot choose a caste for oneself.

Dharma—Religious and moral law that mirrors the eternal cosmic law. It also can be understood as a broad term that reflects the thought and practice of Hinduism itself.

Ganesha—An elephant-headed god. He is the son of Shiva.

Henotheism—Belief in and worship of a single god, while recognizing that other gods exist. A type of polytheism.

Karma—The debt a person owes to the universe for bad actions. By doing good deeds, the debt of karma is erased. The goal is to do enough good so that you escape the cycle of reincarnation. This only happens once your karma is completely dissolved.

Kshatriyas—The warrior class of the caste system. Many military and government leaders were part of this caste, as were many of the maharajas, or ruling princes, in India's history.

Moksha—Escape from the cycle of reincarnation after eliminating the debt of karma through right deeds.

Nirvana—Becoming one with the cosmos after achieving moksha. It is not understood as a physical place but an integration of the individual's soul into the cosmos.

Polytheism—A belief in multiple gods.

Shiva—The god of blessing and destruction. He exists in many forms corresponding to the ebb and flow of the cycles of the Hindu system.

Shruti—The part of Hindu scripture that Hindus mainly hear someone say or sing aloud. The Shruti include the four Vedas, which consist largely of hymns to the gods.

Smriti—These texts are not as inspired as the Shruti, but they help Hindus remember the truths of religion.

Sudras—The lowest and largest level of the caste system. Traditionally, these individuals served those of the higher levels of society. If they executed their duties well, their karma would decrease. Then they would be reborn into a higher caste in the next life.

Trimurti—The "trinity" of Hinduism that includes Brahma, Vishnu, and Shiva.

Vaishyas—The third level of the caste system. Comprised mainly of merchants, farmers, and artisans, the Vaishyas produced the goods consumed by society as a whole. Most menial tasks were left to the Sudras, though.

Vishnu—Defender of the eternal law of the Absolute. He exists in many avatars, or descents, such as Krishna.

Buddhism

Disenchantment led a young Hindu prince named Siddhartha Gautama to abandon a world of comfort at the palace. His father gave him everything he could have wanted, including three palaces and thousands of dancing girls, yet something was missing. The more he experienced life outside the palace, the more he realized that his existence was hollow and meaningless. His marriage at the age of sixteen didn't help, nor did the birth of a son. At the age of twenty-nine, Siddhartha clothed himself in yellow — the color many **ascetic*** monks in his area wore — and slipped out of the palace. By doing so, he renounced his wealth, family, and power to search for spiritual enlightenment.

His quest took many different roads, but in the end, Siddhartha, known to us as **Buddha***, apparently experienced the enlightenment he desperately sought. His life became the foundation of a global religion: Buddhism. Those following the Buddhist worldview seek to attain the perfection in life that Buddha found.

A LIFE OF BUDDHA

While there is no doubt that Siddhartha Gautama was a historical person, researchers find it difficult to get at the actual events of his life. Part of the problem is that the life and sayings of Buddha were passed orally from one monk to another for several centuries before they were recorded in the third century BC. From what we can tell, around 563 BC, Queen Maya gave birth to Siddhartha.[1] According to one legend, just before giving birth, Queen Maya dreamed that a white elephant entered her body. She understood this as a positive omen that her son would be endowed with special powers and strength. When

Maya gave birth, Siddhartha supposedly stood up, took seven steps, and proclaimed, "I have been born to achieve awakening for the good of the world: this is my last birth."[2]

There are multiple accounts of his childhood and early years, including his marriage. In almost all stories, Siddhartha's father was extremely worried that his son would be tainted by the evil in the world. Because of this, he sheltered Siddhartha from the world around him.

According to tradition, the gods looked down on Siddhartha's sheltered existence and sought to awaken him to the reality of human existence. They gave him four visions, or "sights," that planted the seeds of disenchantment in his heart. The first vision was of an old man, the second of a diseased person, and the third was of a dead man being carried to a funerary pyre. Siddhartha had never known aging, disease, or death under his father's protection.

These experiences plunged Siddhartha into a deep depression until he met a calm ascetic dressed in yellow sitting under a tree. In this fourth vision, the monk approached him and explained the road to true peace. The monk informed Siddhartha that peace comes only by embracing aging, disease, and death.

GOING FORTH

To his family's chagrin, Siddhartha donned the yellow robes of the ascetic and left behind the world he had known for thirty years. Even today, the **Pravrajya***, or Siddhartha's departure from his father's home, is reenacted every time a young boy leaves his family to enter a Buddhist monastery.

Free from the bondage of his upbringing, Siddhartha sought a teacher from whom he could learn. He first followed a teacher who stressed meditation as the way to true peace. Siddhartha did not discover enlightenment through this path. The second teacher emphasized renunciation of bodily desires. Siddhartha restricted his diet to one grain of rice per day and slept on a bed of thorns. He followed this extreme until he became skin and bones. He even refused to bathe, letting the dirt fall off his body when it was too heavy to stick to his skin.

His adherence to the teaching he received did nothing but make him weak. After passing out on the edge of a riverbank, he determined that true enlightenment would not be found with extreme **asceticism***. He got up, accepted a bowl of rice offered by a young girl, and ate. His few disciples left in disgust. Self-indulgence would never produce enlightenment, they thought. The future Buddha disagreed. He vowed to find a Middle Way between the two extremes. Refreshed from his meal, he wandered for some time seeking the Middle Way.

AWAKENINGS

> For ever am I liberated,
> This is the last time that I'm born,
> No new existence waits for me.[3]

Exhausted from his wanderings, Siddhartha finally sat down under the **Bodhi Tree***. He determined to meditate until he had answers to his questions. As he fell into his trancelike state, the evil **deva*** Mara, the god who governed **samsara*** — the process of reincarnation — tried to distract him from his meditation. Mara sent his sons to kill Siddhartha and his daughters to seduce him, but nothing could break his peaceful state. Mara then released all of his armies to attack Siddhartha. Without breaking out of his meditative state, Siddhartha simply touched the ground, and the earth goddess caused the ground to vibrate. Mara's frightened warriors retreated.

Siddhartha continued to meditate into the night. As the night went on, he finally attained enlightenment about the **dharma***, or law, of human existence. At the first light of dawn, Siddhartha became Buddha, the enlightened or awakened one. No longer tied to the cycle of reincarnation, Buddha announced his victory with a loud roar.

THE GREAT WHEEL IS SPINNING

For the next seven weeks, Buddha meditated on his new awareness. He decided that the knowledge he had attained was meant to be shared with all people. He traveled some one hundred miles from his place of enlightenment and found his former students in a deer park near Varanasi in northeastern India. He told his former companions about the "First Turning of the Dharma Wheel." From this point forward, he spent the remainder of his life preaching along the roads of northern India, attracting many disciples. At the age of eighty, he ate food provided by a blacksmith where he was teaching. The food made him sick. For a few days he traveled, but eventually he lay down on his right side between two trees and entered into a meditative trance. When he finally died, a Buddhist tradition tells that the entire universe shook. Though enlightened as a man, Buddha had finally attained **nirvana***, the eternal blissful state, never to be reborn again.

THE DHARMA OF BUDDHA

The foundation of Buddhism can be found in the "Four Noble Truths" Buddha taught in his first sermon. At this point, it may be helpful to remember that the purpose of Buddhism is to escape samsara, or reincarnation. That is where true nirvana is found. Buddha's teachings are thought to be a guide on the path to ultimate nirvana, which may not be gained in a Buddhist's lifetime but will hopefully be attained at some point during a future life.

Buddha taught that life is full of sorrow and pain. Remember how Siddhartha's father shielded him from any experiences with aging, disease, or death? Buddha believed true enlightenment can be found only by embracing the reality of death and decay along with suffering during life. In fact, he believed the things that produce happiness are simply an illusion. Humans deceive themselves into thinking that pain can be escaped. By embracing suffering, a person can begin the path toward nirvana.

Next, Buddha taught that any suffering was the direct result of clinging to the impermanent world. Everything we see and experience around us is temporary; it is passing away. Possessions, ideas, and feelings come and go. Even friends and family eventually pass away. Buddha taught that the stuff of life is impermanent and not real. By holding on to the "unreal," we cause ourselves unnecessary suffering. This even includes holding on to the concept of "self." A person's self is only a conglomeration of energy, memories, and human emotions. If we view even ourselves as more than a passing thing, we can't help falling prey to useless activities that are destructive to society. We'll talk more about this concept later when we look at what is called the Noble Eightfold Path.

Buddha's third teaching insists that the final release from suffering is found by distancing ourselves from desire. Despite the abuses his body underwent before he experienced enlightenment, he argued that unless a person dies to selfish desires, there can be no nirvana. During this stage, a person learns to cultivate wisdom. This wisdom allows a person to see into the realities of life—suffering, impermanence, and the need to disavow self and desire. If a person can master these three teachings of Buddha, then it's possible to experience nirvana.

The fourth idea Buddha taught his followers is an ethical way of life. Called the Noble Eightfold Path, Buddha gave a practical system that would speed people's way to nirvana. The eight elements help to define the lifestyle of a true Buddhist and form the practical outworkings of the Buddhist worldview. The eight elements are:

1. Right Understanding: believing the Four Noble Truths and the rest of Buddha's teaching.

2. Right Thought: committing oneself to the discipline necessary to bring every thought into captivity so that a person becomes free from lust, untruthfulness, and self.

3. Right Speech: speaking only true words. In addition, only gracious words freed from the prison of self should be expressed.

4. Right Action: five basic ethical prescriptions: no intentional destruction of life; no stealing; no forced sex; no lying; no intoxication.

5. Right Livelihood: choosing a vocation that gives proper financial support but doesn't violate any other proscriptions. For example, a Buddhist would think twice before becoming a soldier because he would have to kill other humans, and that would involve intentional destruction of life.

6. Right Effort: drawing from the energies inside of a person to force the mind to focus and meditate despite distractions.

7. Right Mindfulness: examining every thought or emotion, because we are a product of our thoughts.

8. Right Concentrations: emptying the mind and allowing it to rest. In this deep state of meditation, the final stage is realized when one neither feels at ease nor upset.

If a person follows all of the steps of the Four Noble Truths, including the Noble Eightfold Path, then that person may experience nirvana. If nirvana is attained, the **arahat***, or the person who escapes the cycle of samsara, no longer is subject to turmoil of mind and begins to experience a oneness with the universe.

KARMA POLICE
A concept called **karma*** forms the basis for the attainment of nirvana. Although there are nuanced differences between Hindu and Buddhist ideas of karma, for our purposes we can consider them similar. Simply put, karma is the force thought to govern the cycle of samsara. In other words, a person's actions will determine the karma she experiences. If she chooses to do immoral things, she should expect karmic demerits. At death, that person will be reborn as a lower life-form. A person who lives a moral life increases the merit she experiences. It follows then that a good person can expect a higher level of rebirth in the next life. Hopefully, in each rebirth, she learns to do better. When her good karma exceeds her bad karma, she is closer to experiencing nirvana.

In most Buddhist teachings, the only way to truly attain nirvana would be to live as a Buddhist monk. Being a monk doesn't guarantee nirvana but separates you from the pressures of the outside world so that it's easier to gain final freedom. Those who aren't monks find hope by living a good life so that at the next rebirth, they are born as a monk. Since women can't be monks, they too must hope for reincarnation as a man who enters a Buddhist monastery.

TWO BRANCHES

Buddhism, like most other religions, has many branches or denominations. The two dominant strands are the **Theravada*** and **Mahayana***. The divisions in Buddhism sprouted just after Buddha's death. By the third century BC, there were approximately seventeen different schools of thought. Both the Theravada and Mahayana schools of interpretation are the direct result of the continued fracturing of the religion between 200 BC and AD 200.

Theravada Buddhists hold to the strictest expression of Buddhism that is closer to what Buddha taught.[4] These Buddhists believe that nirvana is attained by following the Buddha's teaching. They emphasize the Pali Canon of scriptures written about 80 BC as the purest expression of what Buddha taught. Also called the **Tripitaka***, or the Three Baskets, this bible for Theravada Buddhists is about ten times larger than the Christian Bible.

The Mahayana tradition emphasizes many of the oral traditions and myths that broadened the ideas present in Buddha's teaching. Mahayana means the "great vehicle," as this branch has a much broader view of salvation. When Mahayana Buddhists talk about nirvana, they emphasize that the wisest of all individuals would not actually experience nirvana, because he would stay to help those who had not yet attained enlightenment. Nirvana is understood simply as a state of spiritual perfection. They hold that there have been many Buddhas in history, all of them coming as divine teachers who were manifestations of the Absolute. Buddha himself was not really a man, but an illusion who appeared so that men would hear the message given by the divine Absolute. Because of this, Mahayanas often worship Buddha as a god. This worship is an affront to the beliefs of Theravada Buddhists.

NOW AND ZEN

Zen Buddhism, popularized in the West through Japanese traditions and in movies like *Crouching Tiger, Hidden Dragon*, emphasizes the power of meditation. This tradition reached its full definition around AD 520. Zen Buddhists stress the teaching of enlightened masters who have come before and shared their teachings. Many of these teachings were written after the scriptures held sacred by the Theravada or Mahayana traditions. At the core of its teaching, Zen stresses four elements: the power of its enlightened teachers, the power of experience instead of scripture, the power of meditation, and the power of internal examination that leads to enlightenment.

DIAMONDS IN THE ROUGH

The last Buddhist tradition we will look at is known as the diamond vehicle, or Tantric Buddhism. Tantric Buddhists believe that their system can allow a person to escape samsara in only one lifetime. They believe their methods can cut through even the toughest layers of unbelief and ignorance. Through the powerful teachings of a **siddha***, or saint, people come to enlightenment. These saints teach that the only reality is the Absolute.

Tantric Buddhism, more than any other branch, merges traditional folk deities into the practice of Buddhism. It combines beliefs about magic, spells, demons, and gods into its spiritual practice. It emphasizes the godlike nature of each individual as he or she seeks to attain oneness with the Absolute through meditation.[5]

For those following the diamond vehicle, the goal is to remove all elements of dualism because the Absolute is the one force in the cosmos. Since there is only one force, Tantric Buddhists believe there is no such thing as male or female. In fact, each person possesses both feminine and masculine elements. The masculine elements express themselves through external acts while the feminine aspects are demonstrated by the ability to focus inward.

This form of Buddhism has received great attention over the past decade or so because of the prominence of the Dalai Lama in Western culture. Tantric Buddhism in its Tibetan expression venerates spiritual leaders as lamas, or teachers. Tibetan Buddhists believe these gurus are specially reincarnated leaders who continue to be reborn for the sake of the community. Before death, a lama will give signs to his followers of how and where his next reincarnation will take place. When the lama dies, his followers track these signs into the community to find boys of the appropriate age. Those boys who are candidates to be the lama are presented with several objects. If the boy consistently chooses several items that the prior lama regularly used, the monks take him to the monastery as the reincarnation of the lama.

WORLDVIEW SIGNPOSTS

Now that you have a general idea of how Buddhism works and what Buddhists believe, let's look at our six points of comparison.

God

While Buddhists as a whole don't believe in a God as the monotheistic faiths do, all branches of Buddhism recognize the reality
of supernatural beings such as gods and demons. These beings
aren't deities to be worshiped, but transient beings much like
humans. In the cycle of samsara, a Buddhist could conceivably
be reborn as a deity, only to be reborn later as a lower life-form
such as an animal.

Buddhists recognize a concept of the Absolute, or a unifying cosmic force in the universe. Much like Brahman in
Hinduism, the Absolute is the only true reality recognized. If
you want to escape the cycle of samsara, you follow the teachings of Buddha, and eventually you experience nirvana, joining
with the Absolute and assimilating yourself into it.

Mahayana, Zen, and Tantric Buddhism elevate Buddha to
near-divine or divine status. Because of this, many Buddhists
worship him as a god. They pray and offer sacrifices to Buddha
statues or even Buddhist "saints." For many lay Buddhists, it's
hard to distinguish between the man Buddha and the concept
of Buddha as a god.

Humanity

Buddhists place a high value on life. They believe every person
possesses deep within himself the ability to achieve enlightenment and experience nirvana. While this may not happen in
one lifetime, continued dedication to attaining nirvana will
cause a person's karmic merits to exceed his karmic demerits so
that he can escape samsara.

Despite stressing that every human has the capability to
attain freedom from the cycle of reincarnation, Buddhism
doesn't elevate humans above other animals. All life is equally

valuable, which means a dog or a cow has the same amount of karmic presence as a man or a woman. Because all forms of life contain value and Buddhists must never knowingly take life, many are vegetarians.

Salvation

Salvation is available to everyone, because anyone can experience nirvana if he chooses to walk the path of Buddha. Karma is an important factor. Based upon the ethics of the Noble Eightfold Path, a person earns good karma for good deeds and demerits for bad behavior. When good karma exceeds demerits, a person comes closer to nirvana. It may take several lifetimes to attain complete freedom, but the Buddhist must continue to press forward in each lifetime if he is ever going to attain the ultimate freedom.

The concept of karma can be a difficult one for many to follow. Many people grow frustrated and feel entrapped by negative karma they believe they experienced in a prior lifetime. Working out salvation in this lifetime takes work, time, and dedication in the Buddhist system. The process extends beyond this lifetime and may require multiple rebirths to achieve final nirvana. No wonder Buddha was said to roar in victory when he attained enlightenment!

Authority

The teachings of Buddha are the authority of Buddhism. Unfortunately, for almost three hundred years, these were only communicated orally, passed from monk to monk. Buddhists believe that the true teachings of Buddha were preserved in these transmissions and eventually recorded in what is called a **sutra*** (plural: **suttas***). The Pali Canon, written around 80 BC, contains the Theravada scriptures. It has three sections that are often referred to as the Three Baskets: the teachings of Buddha, rules for monks, and interpretations of the dharma of Buddha.

The Mahayana scriptures are much larger and vary in size depending on the country. In China alone, more than five thousand authoritative volumes exist. Often the writings of these suttas may be worshiped instead of the statue of a Buddha since they are equated with Buddha's teaching. The Mahayana Buddhists also continue to add to the corpus of writings. The basic idea is that the dharma, or teaching, contained in these scriptures is only recorded to help people get beyond their suffering. One author put it this way:

> When people use a raft to cross a river, they leave the raft behind and go on their way. When someone uses the Dharma to cross the river of suffering, the words of the Dharma can be left behind.[6]

To further complicate matters, remember that the Zen and Tantric branches believe in the authority of their teachers, not in written suttas. Their authority can be based on personal life experience, which teaches as much as any sutra.

Time

You have probably picked up by now that heaven is not a literal place for Buddhists. Instead, Buddhists search for eternal nirvana. Since a person is reborn multiple times until she experiences nirvana, most Buddhists don't understand the idea of a literal heaven or hell. Even if you were to attain nirvana in the Buddhist system, you would simply never be reborn. You would join the Absolute in a perfect state of awareness and oneness. Some Buddhists have argued that you simply cease to exist after nirvana is attained.

Jesus

Since Buddha lived several centuries before Christ, the writings of the Pali Canon don't address Jesus. He is simply thought of among Buddhists as a great spiritual leader, an incarnation of Buddha or a **bodhisattva***. Some people even try to worship Jesus together with Buddha. One Buddhist teacher wrote to Christians about how he worships Jesus *and* Buddha:

> I put a lot of Buddha statues on my altar, about ten or fifteen very small Buddhas one centimeter high and larger ones too. I also have a statue of Jesus as my ancestor. I have adopted Jesus Christ as one of my spiritual ancestors.[7]

In many cases, Jesus is spiritualized to the point where he is either part of the Absolute or present in the teachings of Buddha or the Bible. One monk wrote that "Jesus is born every time the Holy Spirit in you is touched."[8] While this is consistent with Buddhist teachings, it doesn't take into account the teachings of Christ.

BUDDHISM AND CHRISTIANITY

The Buddhist worldview continues to grow in influence as it spreads across America and much of the West. Hollywood actors such as Richard Gere and Harrison Ford have accepted forms of Buddhism as their personal religion. Zen Buddhism filters into many yoga centers and karate studios. Even Lisa

Simpson in a 2001 Christmas episode of the popular TV show *The Simpsons* became a Buddhist.

Buddhism also appeals to many people who care for the environment and value all life, including animals. Many of the statements of leaders in groups such as PETA (People for the Ethical Treatment of Animals) sound close to Buddhist teachings.

In addition, many people who believe vaguely in tolerance find in Buddhism a way for everyone to get along peacefully. Buddhism's acceptance of multiple paths to nirvana leads naturally to tolerance. Many people find comfort in Buddha's teaching that each person is on her own path. Everybody must discover his own personal way to nirvana. This idea leads to the practice of syncretism, which we will discuss later in this book (page 193).

Buddhism puts the individual in charge of her own destiny. This approach appeals to Westerners for whom the freedom of personal choice is one of the highest values. Ironically, though, while the individual chooses her path, the goal of the journey is to cease to be an individual, to join with the Absolute and have one's self extinguished. By contrast, Islam and Christianity are far less "tolerant," because both religions insist that they offer the only true path. God, not the individual, is in charge. Islam asks the individual to submit to God, and Christianity asks her to accept the forgiveness offered only through the work of Christ. Yet the goal of both of these religions keeps the individual soul intact.

If Jesus had read Buddha's teachings, he would have agreed with some of the core ideas. Jesus taught by word and example that suffering is inevitable in life, and that one should use it for God's purposes rather than try to escape it. He embraced a path of suffering that led to his brutal death when he could have escaped it. Jesus also agreed that clinging to life's impermanent things, such as possessions or status, is a recipe for a wasted life. Yet some of the things that Buddha said are impermanent, Jesus said are not. For Jesus, every individual human self is eternal. He trained his followers to increasingly say no to their selfish desires so they could say yes to the desire to know God personally. Buddha would say the desire to know God is an illusion.

Buddha taught that people are reborn over and over in new bodies until they can escape the wheel of karma. Jesus taught that people live and die once in one body, and after that they face God. Buddhists and Christians can live side by side respectfully with these dramatically different beliefs, but these views of life and death can't both be true. Either we are reborn over and over, or we aren't. Tolerance that agrees not to disrespect or kill each other over disagreements is possible and desirable, but tolerance that says the disagreements are unimportant is disrespectful to both religions.

Despite the diversity found in the various expressions of Buddhism, the basic worldview remains the same: Enlightenment is the way forward for all of humanity. Live a good life so that you can experience true nirvana sometime in this life or the next.

BUDDHISM GLOSSARY

Arahat—A person considered worthy to attain nirvana and escape the cycle of samsara. Arahats are not Buddhas, but people who, by following the Four Noble Truths, have reached true nirvana.

Asceticism—A belief in denying bodily appetites for food, sex, physical comfort, and so on, for spiritual purposes. Usually the term is used for more than moderate self-denial.

Bodhi Tree—The Tree of Enlightenment where Siddhartha finally attained enlightenment. This tree is often pictured in Buddhist art behind the image of Buddha sitting in the lotus position (legs crossed).

Bodhisattva—One on the path to become a Buddha. Literally means "a Buddha-to-be."

Buddha—An enlightened or awakened one. Though the historical person Buddha may have been the first to experience enlightenment, there are others who are also Buddhas who experience perfect nirvana as well.

Deva—A supernatural being, a god. They are as impermanent as humans and are subject to the laws of reincarnation as well.

Dharma—Truth or law as found in the teachings of Buddha.

Karma—The laws that govern samsara, or reincarnation. Karma determines how a person will be reborn.

Mahayana—The northern form of Buddhism found in China, Korea, Japan, Tibet, and Mongolia. The name literally means "great vehicle" (as opposed to Theravada Buddhism). This form of Buddhism deifies Buddha and stresses the broad way of salvation.

Nirvana—The perfect enlightenment only attainable at death by a Buddha who escapes samsara. It is a perfect eternal state completely outside the realm of time where a person's soul is like a drop of water returning to the ocean.

Pravrajya—Buddha's "going forth" from his family to seek ultimate truth.

Samsara—The cycle of life that goes from birth to death and leads to reincarnation.

Siddha—A saint or an accomplished teacher in Tantric Buddhism.

Sutra (plural: suttas)—A teaching by Buddha recorded by a monk.

Theravada—A dominant branch of Buddhism that emphasizes the teaching of the elders. It is one of the oldest streams of Buddhist interpretation and is prevalent in Sri Lanka, Thailand, and Burma. It is often referred to as the "small vehicle" of salvation, as it stresses strict adherence to Buddha's teaching as the only way to nirvana.

Tripitaka—The Three Baskets of the Pali Canon, or scriptures, that the Theravada Buddhists follow.

Islam

A quick quiz question: What is the fastest growing religion in the Western world? Christianity? No. Buddhism or New Age? Nope. The correct answer: Islam. Despite the actions of a small group of Islamic radicals that sponsor terrorism, Islam continues to attract new converts at a rate unmatched by other groups.[1] The reality is the radicals who dominate much of the evening news are a very small minority of a religion that many believe gives them purpose and meaning. Let's begin with a little history about Muhammad.

THE BIRTH OF A PROPHET

By all accounts, **Muhammad*** entered the world in the worst situation. His father died a couple of months before his birth, stranding Muhammad and his mother without any financial support. Muhammad grew up in abject poverty until he reached the age of six, when his mother died. His grandfather and uncle took him to live with them. The **Koran*** states it this way:

> Did He [Allah] not find you an orphan and give
>   you shelter?
> And He found you wandering, and He gave you
>   guidance.
> And He found you in need, and made you
>   independent. **Sura*** 93:6-8

Regardless of how the story is told, Muhammad and his visions from the angels of **Allah*** formed a new religion in the seventh century that would become one of the largest belief systems in the world. In this chapter, we are going to explore **Islam*** and its unique, monotheistic worldview.

Before we begin, some clarification is in order. The word *Islam* is taken from an Arabic term that means both submission and peace. By definition, to follow the religion of Islam is the peaceful, wholehearted surrender to the leadership and direction of Allah. A **Muslim***, derived from the same family of words, is "one who submits" to the teachings of Allah. Muslims believe the Koran is the recorded words of Allah spoken through the prophet Muhammad. Since the Koran is the revelation of God, it is considered holy. We'll talk more about the Koran in a bit.

MUHAMMAD'S LIFE

Despite some of the hardship of Muhammad's early life, his grandfather and uncle ensured that he got a traditional education and training as a merchant. Around the age of twenty-five, he began to work for one of the more powerful regional merchants by the name of Khadija. Muhammad's devotion and ethics impressed her. The two of them eventually married (even though Khadija was fifteen years older than Muhammad), and Muhammad helped her manage her large trading business.

Muhammad turned forty sometime around AD 610 (we don't know his precise date of birth). He left home to trade near Mecca in Saudi Arabia. According to the Koran, he had a vision while staying overnight in a cave. An angel appeared with the command for Muhammad to recite the words he heard. Just as suddenly as the angel materialized, it disappeared. Muhammad said he wrote down the exact words he heard from the angel.

Muhammad worried about the vision. In fact, he feared he was possessed by an evil spirit or demon. When he consulted Khadija, she couldn't answer him and sent him to her uncle, a Christian, to explain the meaning of the message. He told Muhammad that his vision was identical to the Law that had been given to Moses. Muhammad didn't find this answer comforting. In fact, he thought he was crazy.[2] He retreated to the desert to try to sort out what was happening.

While in the desert, he had another vision. This time, the angel that appeared identified himself as Gabriel, the messenger of Allah. Muhammad fell into a trance and reportedly began to speak words that were not his own. When he awoke from his trance, he wrote down the words he remembered from his vision. He realized that he was a new prophet, a mouthpiece of Allah to his people. He believed that these revelations were designed to be scripture for his tribe and family.

He continued to receive visions for several years. At the same time, he tried to convince family and friends of this new message from Allah. His first converts were his family, including his wife. Others soon followed. Many of these first followers of Islam were young men from other wealthy families who were impressed by Muhammad's life. But many people rejected his message because he was attacking the traditional gods. Some area tribal leaders even tried to kill him.

During this time of persecution, he had another vision in which he visited Jerusalem. In his dream he met with Abraham, Moses, and Jesus. He even led them in prayer. After he prayed, Gabriel took him to view the seven heavens. Muslims later built the Dome of the Rock in Jerusalem to commemorate Muhammad's ascent to heaven.

After this experience, Muhammad felt a new boldness to preach the message of submission to the one God, Allah. This further irritated those who were persecuting Muhammad and his followers. They attacked his family and followers, forcing them to flee from Mecca to Medina.

In Medina he acquired new converts, and the religion grew more rapidly than before. The elders of Medina surrendered control of their city and asked Muhammad to lead them. He used his visions to teach the people how to live in submission to Allah. He stressed that true believers in Allah form an **umma***, or a unique community. For followers of Allah to live good lives, everyone needed the accountability of a community.

Eventually Muhammad returned to Mecca, but this time with an army. He quickly subdued those who had opposed him. According to Islamic tradition, he demonstrated the mercy of Allah by stopping his army before any blood was shed. Astonished, the people of Mecca willingly listened to his message of Islam, and many converted.

On June 8, 632, Muhammad died after a long illness. By the time of his death, he had created a new religion and a new worldview in the deserts of the East. This new worldview centered on submission to a monotheistic god, Allah. It placed Muhammad as the final prophet of Allah, and stressed that the Koran was a perfect revelation from Allah. Muhammad also introduced an orderly and ethical way of life to the many tribes that had held different standards. He mandated a lifestyle of prayer and fasting as signs of submission to Allah. Muslims still visit his grave in Medina and remember the message he brought to the people.

ISLAM AFTER MUHAMMAD

Muhammad never established a succession of leadership before he died. As his followers sought to maintain community devotion to the Koran, a division broke out between those who desired a leader from Muhammad's family and those who wanted one who demonstrated a holy lifestyle. The solution was the appointment of the first **caliph***, Abu Bakr, Muhammad's father-in-law and one of the very first converts.

Future leaders came to be known as caliphs, which meant that they were considered deputies of Muhammad. The caliphs served as both religious and political leaders. Under their leadership, Islam spread from Spain to India within one hundred years of Muhammad's death.

After securing these broad boundaries, Islam flowered intellectually, with explosive development in the arts, math, and sciences. According to historical records, Muslims were the first to use anesthesia in surgery and to have mobile hospital clinics, which were carried on the backs of camels.[3] Their architecture flourished, and the characteristic geometrical designs of Islamic art reached their height. Islamic poetry and literature rivaled anything in the West. In short, Islam became a major cultural force, especially when compared with the declining Christianity of the West, where heresy and internal political battles weakened the church.

With its rapid growth and high culture, Islam positioned itself as a force to be reckoned with. The image of the crescent and star still found on every mosque indicates Muhammad's personal understanding that Islam was a universal religion that was to extend from the earth to the moon. He believed that Islam revealed truths that would guide all of humanity into true life, submission, and holiness.

THE MAIN BRANCHES

The debate over the succession of leadership after Muhammad birthed Islam's two main branches, the **Sunnis*** and the

Shi'ites*. Today there are multiple groups that claim to hold to the true interpretation of Islam, but the Sunnis and the Shi'ites comprise more than 90 percent of all Muslims worldwide.

The division occurred when Muhammad's son-in-law Ali was appointed as the fourth caliph. Some argued that the true successor of Muhammad's message would be chosen because of his sincere faith and belief, not necessarily because of his relation to the prophet. The group who took this view became known as the Sunnis. Another group believed that the successor to Muhammad must be of direct lineage to the prophet. The Shi'ites maintain this belief even today.

Sunnis are the largest branch of Muslims. They are more moderate in their interpretation of the Koran and stress the role of tradition. This became crucial for the Muslim community as they sought to deal with difficult questions that the Koran did not address specifically. In these cases, early Sunnis looked to the example of Muhammad first. If they didn't find an answer, they sought the consensus of the Medina community. If there was still no clear direction, the Sunnis followed the tradition of their local community. In their interpretations, Sunnis bind the civil law and the Koran together tightly. In other words, for a Sunni Muslim, the laws of the government and those given in the Koran ought to be one and the same. They believe passionately that Islam presents the **Shari'a***, or the true path of religion that encompasses every area of life.

Shi'ites approach the Koran in a different way. Instead of appealing to tradition, Shi'ites take the Koran very literally. They emphasize the importance of living a saintly life and stress that perfection is attainable in this life. As a result, they believe that Allah will hold each individual accountable for his or her own actions.

THE FIVE PILLARS OF ISLAM

Islam is as complex as any religious system, involving a broad range of groups that interpret the Koran in a variety of different ways. But in every branch of Islam, there are five common beliefs that every Muslim must follow. These **Five Pillars*** capture the heart of Islamic teaching, upon which the entire religion and worldview are built.

1. Unity—The claim, "There is no god but Allah, and Muhammad is his prophet," is the heart of Islamic faith. This statement provides the unity for the entire Islamic worldview. Called the **shahadah***, or the witness of the faith, this profession is said to be so powerful that making this claim and believing in it is enough to make anyone a Muslim. Of course, since Islam is a whole system of right belief and submission to Allah, the shahadah must be followed by obeying the other tenets of Islam.

2. Prayer—Following the example of Muhammad, the true Muslim prays five times daily facing Mecca. The interjection of prayer into daily life is designed to remind Muslims of their rightful place of obedience before Allah—a place of submission. As they pray, Muslims vary their posture by standing, kneeling, and bowing before Allah at various times during the daily prayers. All of these positions follow what Muhammad taught his followers and have been practiced since the beginning of Islam. The daily prayers are offered in the fields, in a place of business, or wherever the person finds himself. Many people go to the mosque to pray. In fact, the word *mosque* derives from an Arabic term meaning "a place of prostration," which reflects the positions Muslims take during prayer.[4]

3. Giving—Muhammad set the example for all Muslims by giving generously out of his wealth. Because of this, all Muslims are expected to give at least one-fortieth of their income to purify the earnings in the eyes of God. They usually give this gift to the mosque for distribution to the poor and needy in the Islamic community.

4. Fasting—During the month of Ramadan, when Muslims celebrate the giving of the Koran to Muhammad, all believers fast. This daily fast from food, drink, and sexual activity begins at the first moment of dawn and doesn't end until the sun sets. At the end of the month, the community celebrates with a large festival where families bring the money they saved from food expenditures during the month to distribute to the poor.

5. Pilgrimage—It is expected that every Muslim, if he is healthy, will make a spiritual pilgrimage to Mecca at least once in his life. Those who are too poor to make the journey are excused from this portion of the pillars. Instead, they can contribute to a fund to allow others to make a pilgrimage.

To these Five Pillars is also added the concept of **jihad***. In our day, jihad has become synonymous with the holy war of Islamic extremists, but the term originally meant vigorously applying oneself to the teachings of the Koran. It was considered jihad to perform the Five Pillars or simply to die to oneself in order to submit to Allah. In this regard, jihad is a day-to-day activity.

According to one writer, the vast majority of Muslims consider jihad as "vigilance against all that distracts us from God and exertion to do his will."[5] The problem with extremists is they take this mandate and twist it. They portray Western culture and ideas as significant threats to Islamic faith and practice. Therefore, in the rationale of the Islamic extremists, it's valid to attack the West and its people because the Western way of life is distracting Muslims from the true practice of Islam.

WORLDVIEW SIGNPOSTS

Now that we have covered some of the basics about Islam, let's turn to examine the six signposts of our worldview map and see what Islam teaches.

God

"There is no god but Allah, and Muhammad is his prophet." This claim, called the shahadah, sets out the main identification of Islam's monotheism. The Koran continues, "There is no god but He, the Creator of all things."[6] This claim, along with others in the Koran, has caused many well-meaning people to equate Allah with the God of the Bible. In terms of simple definition—*Allah* literally means "the god"—this is true. However, neither the Koran nor the teachings of other monotheistic religions agree beyond this simple point. In fact, a significant gulf exists between Allah and the God of Judaism or Christianity. Let's talk about a few concepts that Muslims hold when they talk about Allah.

Muslims believe in Allah as the one god. This idea is repeated daily in the prayers of Muslims all over the world. It also makes perfect sense in light of the first pillar we discussed above. It also reflects Muhammad's dislike of the pagan religions of his day. As a merchant, Muhammad was well acquainted with Judaism, Christianity, and other religions of the Arabian Peninsula. Most disturbing to him were the ancient tribal religions.

Many of these tribal religions, including the traditions of his family, placed an emphasis on beings or gods who controlled the weather or were represented by animals. According to one tradition, Muhammad's grandfather was willing to offer Muhammad's father as a burnt sacrifice to gain the approval of the gods. Instead, a fortuneteller encouraged Muhammad's grandfather to redeem his son by offering a hundred camels in his place.[7] If he had offered the son, Muhammad would never have been born. No wonder he disliked the pagan rituals and deities!

Muslims are very careful in their speech about Allah. To name Allah is to define god, which is impossible, because he is without limit. In all, the Koran reveals ninety-nine names of Allah that believers can use. These range from Allah as Judge to Allah as Merciful. Many Muslims carry a small beaded bracelet that contains ninety-nine beads to remind them of the names that Allah revealed about himself.

The main difference between Allah and the God of Judaism and Christianity is that Allah does not enter into a personal relationship with his creatures. In the Bible, God met and spoke with Abraham and the prophets, he referred to David as a man after his own heart, and he personally called the apostle Paul into his service. Christianity calls humanity into personal relationship with God through Jesus Christ. In the Koran, Allah does not engage humanity on a personal level. He even sends angels to Muhammad to dictate the Koran instead of meeting with him personally.

As the god without limits according to Islamic writings, Allah is an awe-inspiring being who doesn't stoop to bother himself with the inanities of human life and existence. He is the great god above all else to whom none could ever aspire to reach. As the righteous judge, he hands out mercy, grace, death, and judgment from his heavenly throne.[8] As such, Allah has no personal relationship with humans. He is so completely other that to do so would lessen his magnificence. As Muslims continue to submit to Allah as the highest being, only then do they begin to experience his presence in the world around them.[9]

Despite the inability of humans to have a personal relationship with Allah, Muslims do believe that they can approach him with requests through prayer. During moments of prayer, men and women enter into Allah's presence to seek his favor. This occurs without any intermediary between the Muslim and Allah. Still, humans are Allah's servants or slaves, not people with whom he wants to build relationships.

One small group within the Muslim world teaches that Allah can be experienced on a personal level. This branch of Islam, **Sufism***, stresses the aspects of love and pure religion. Known as a mystical sect of Islam, Sufis understand their lives as a lamp from which the light of Allah can shine. They equate prayer with Muhammad's trip through the heavens where one can meet with Allah one-on-one. However popular this branch of Islam has been in different periods of history, it has not overturned the orthodox perspective that a personal relationship with Allah is impossible, because humans are simply his servants and cannot know him personally.

Humanity

Humans have two roles in Islam. The first role is servant of Allah. The concept of humanity as servant has huge ramifications in the worldview of all Muslims. They are called to do the bidding of the awesome, all-powerful god. During their regular prayers, Muslims prostrate themselves as slaves before their master. Even the name *Muslim* comes from the idea of submission to Allah.

Even though Muslims are slaves of Allah and are to submit to him, they believe they have a special role on the earth as his administrators of justice and truth. This goes back to the Koranic teaching about creation. Much like the Bible, the Koran emphasizes that humans are the special creation of God. They didn't evolve from lower animals. Humans always have and will be the center of Allah's creative masterpiece. When Adam and Eve ate the forbidden fruit in paradise, both were guilty of sinning against Allah's will. When Adam and Eve sinned, they fell. In Christianity and Judaism, partaking of the forbidden fruit altered the very being of humanity. In Islam, however, the Fall made Adam and Eve forget who Allah really is. Every human since the time of Adam and Eve forgot the reason they were born. Yet embedded deep in the human soul rests an innate understanding of Allah. The job of religion, and Islam in particular, is to help every person "remember" Allah.

According to Muslims, Islam awakens the design that Allah had for humanity at creation. Through submission, the intellect of humanity awakes and fulfills Allah's original command to dominate the earth. Only after being awakened can humans begin to administer the gifts and talents Allah gave to everyone. These gifts remain available to an individual only as long as she remains submitted to Allah. Accordingly, Muslims believe they are to serve as Allah's administrators on earth and are responsible for bringing all of humanity into a right relationship of submission under him.

Islam emphasizes the equality of Allah's servants. Malcolm X, one-time leader of the Nation of Islam, recorded his astonishment at how every pilgrim, whether rich or poor, black or white, was considered and treated as equal:

We were *truly* all the same (brothers)—because their belief in one God had removed the "white" from their *minds*, the "white" from their *behavior*, and the "white" from their *attitude*. I could see from this that perhaps if white Americans could accept the Oneness of God, then perhaps, too, they could accept *in reality* the Oneness of Man—and cease to measure, and hinder, and harm others in terms of their "differences" in color.[10]

Again, Muslims believe they are all simply Allah's servants. The only difference he sees is whether or not a person is submissive.

Salvation

Salvation comes to any person who is willing to believe the shahadah. It is believed that the simple acknowledgement that "there is no god but Allah, and Muhammad is his prophet" is enough to convert anyone to Islam. Once this claim is sincerely made, then the process of submission must begin for the true act of salvation to take place. As we discussed above, Islam holds that every human knows the truth in his heart, so the heart only has to remember the truth it forgot. At that moment of remembering, the heart can confess the shahadah and enter into the community of Islam. Salvation is maintained by continuing to submit to Allah.

Authority

Because Muslims believe in Allah's oneness, they insist the messages he gave through the prophets are the way he reveals his will to humanity. The first prophet was Adam. The last was Muhammad. Between Adam and Muhammad were more than

100,000 prophets who spoke as Allah's mouthpiece at some time. Muslims believe that their god alone chose these prophets and gave them a message to communicate to people at various times.

Allah chose to reveal his final sayings to humanity through Muhammad. The Koran is this final revelation. Muhammad received Allah's words through ecstatic visions. Once Muhammad awoke from these visions, he remembered the messages verbatim and recorded them. Because of this supernatural process, Muslims believe that Muhammad, as the mouthpiece of Allah, recorded the very words of God. Therefore, according to Islam, the Koran contains no errors or human concepts because the revelation was Allah speaking through Muhammad. He simply chose Muhammad as his mouthpiece. Muslims believe the Koran, in its original Arabic, to be perfect in every way.

According to Islam, Allah's ultimate revelation did not happen until Muhammad. Islam honors Jesus and Moses as great prophets. The followers of Moses and Jesus—Jews and Christians—received part of the picture of Allah in their Scriptures, so they are called People of the Book. But because Jews and Christians refuse the final testament to Allah through Muhammad, they can't experience salvation unless they conform to Allah's true will as revealed to Muhammad.

Time

Time began in creation. Muslims believe that Allah created time along with the earth. Someday, Allah will stop time altogether and this world will cease. Muslims will receive a special place in a literal heaven, while those who refuse the message of Allah will suffer in a literal hell.

Sometime after death, all souls will face a final judgment before Allah where each person must give an account of the good or bad deeds he has done. Since every person varies in her level of submission to Allah, heaven has multiple levels where a Muslim will spend eternity. Those who were believers but didn't fully follow the example of Muhammad will dwell in the lowest regions of heaven. The faithful, however, will take pleasure in the highest levels of heaven and enjoy the best food and companionship for all eternity.

Jesus

Jesus appeared on earth as a prophet from God according to the Koran. He came to proclaim that Muhammad was on the way. Muhammad wrote in Sura 61:6,

> And remember, Jesus, the son of Mary said: "Oh Children of Israel! I am the apostle of God [sent] to you confirming the Law [which came] before me, and giving glad Tidings of an Apostle to come after me, whose name shall be Muhammad."

This statement fits the idea that Abraham, Moses, and Jesus foreshadowed the arrival of Allah's final and greatest prophet.

Because Jesus was part of the chain of prophets from Allah, many of his teachings were accepted. In Islamic tradition, Jesus is called the Messiah, which for Muslims simply means prophet. Muslims believe that Gabriel appeared to Mary proclaiming that Christ was coming and that she was a virgin when Jesus was born. At the end of time, they believe Jesus will return to kill the Antichrist and destroy everyone who doesn't believe in Allah and the prophet Muhammad.

Yet Muslims don't believe that Jesus died on the cross, nor that he was resurrected. Instead, an *image* of Jesus appeared on the cross. Jesus' apostles didn't understand what to do after he disappeared, so they invented Christianity. But Muslims believe Christianity misses the point of Jesus' message, which foretold the coming of Islam.

ISLAM AND CHRISTIANITY

In a post–9/11 world, we are confronted with extreme versions of Islam on a daily basis. We feel we need to remind you that not all Muslims are radical terrorists. Most are peace-loving citizens. However, the radical Islamic adherents bring out an important point about the power of a worldview. Why on earth would anyone be willing to kill themselves and others as a statement for their faith? Many of the young men and women who carry out these acts of terrorism fall under the influence of teachers who twist the message of Islam to attain specific political or religious goals. They are taught a warped worldview and believe it. However warped it may be, that worldview allows them to strap bombs to their bodies and set out to attack those who have been portrayed as enemies. Worldviews are powerful things. When we adopt a worldview, it shapes who we are and how we engage the world around us.

The Muslims you are likely to encounter at school or work probably won't be extremists. Still, it will be helpful for you to understand the ways their worldview differs from the Christian one. The essential difference has to do with God's nature. Allah doesn't involve himself personally in human affairs. For Muslims, the idea that Allah would become a man, suffer as a man, and die as a man is crazy or horrible. Many Muslims believe that Christians altered the original New Testament documents to make them say that Jesus was God in human flesh, and that he truly died, was buried, and rose from the dead. There is no historical evidence that Christians altered the New Testament, yet this is a deeply held belief for many Muslims. The Koran affirms the truth of the New Testament, but the New Testament says things about God and Jesus that run counter to Islam, so the theory that the text has been corrupted seems reasonable to many Muslims.

Muslims have great respect for Jesus, but while the Koran affirms some of what the Bible says about him, it rejects aspects that are essential to Christians. The Bible's view of the life, death, and resurrection of Christ—the core of Christian faith—is foreign to Islam.

Likewise, to a Muslim, the Christian idea that God is Father, Son, and Holy Spirit sounds like a belief in three gods. The idea that God is relational in his essence and desires relationship with humans is very hard to square with the picture of Allah in the Koran.

ISLAM GLOSSARY

Allah — The god of Islam. Muslims stress his oneness. He is viewed as the creator, king, and judge of the universe. He is completely separate from humanity and doesn't enter into relationship with any person, but he did speak through specific prophets. He offers grace and mercy to humans if they repent of their wrongdoings and return to the teachings of the Koran.

Caliph — The deputy of the messenger of Allah (Muhammad). A caliph was appointed as the people's political and religious ruler based on the standards of holiness set by the Koran.

Five Pillars — The heart of the Islamic worldview and religion. These Five Pillars of faith summarize the teachings of Muhammad.

Islam — The religion of the people who follow the teachings of Muhammad. They believe that the Koran contains the final teachings of Allah on religion. The word comes from the same root as *Muslim*, one who follows the teachings of Islam and thereby submits to the will of Allah.

Jihad — Jihad originally meant vigorously applying oneself to the teachings of the Koran. It was considered jihad to perform the Five Pillars or simply to die to oneself in order to submit to Allah. In this regard, jihad is a day-to-day activity. Islamic extremists use this word for holy warfare against people who, they believe, distract Muslims from God.

Koran — The holy book of Islam. It is believed to be divinely inspired in its Arabic version. Its pages are believed to contain the final revelation of Allah to humanity.

Muhammad — The prophet of Allah. Muhammad is the one who received the visions and directions from Allah that were written down to form the Koran.

Muslim — A person who has submitted to following Allah and his teachings as revealed through Muhammad in the Koran.

Shahadah — The core belief statement of Islam. "There is no god but Allah, and Muhammad is his prophet." The term *shahadah* derives from the root word for witness.

Shari'a — The Way, or the true path of Islam.

Shi'ites — Members of a branch of Islam that maintains that leadership must come from a descendant of Muhammad. These were the followers of Muhammad's son-in-law Ali.

Sufism — A mystical branch of Islam that seeks to experience God on a personal level.

Sunnis — Members of the majority branch of Islam that reveres the first four caliphs, because they were chosen as leaders by the will of the community. Their name relates to the terms for tradition and custom. Generally speaking, Sunnis treat the Koran more moderately in their interpretation than do Shi'ites. However, many of the modern Islamic extremist groups follow a severe version of Sunni Islam.

Sura — A chapter from the Koran.

Umma — The community of believers in Islam.

3

Naturalism—Worldviews Without God(s)

Naturalism and Materialism
Darwinism
The Sexual Revolution

The world is what we make of it since we are made by it.

Naturalism and Materialism

"100% natural." Or so the label claimed. Nearly every product by this manufacturer featured these words on its label. The idea was to sell you a "natural" product so you'd feel good about purchasing it. If it was "all natural," it had to be better for you, right? But after the products spent a few months on the market, the food company made the news. An independent group of experts examined their claims and found the products were less than natural. In fact, many of the products manufactured by the company contained artificial colors, preservatives, and other additives.

The company defended its products, stating that all of the ingredients other than coloring and preservatives were "all natural." Customers weren't satisfied, and some even sued the company for the false advertising. As you can imagine, the food company lost its case and was fined millions of dollars. As part of the settlement, it revised its labeling to include a disclaimer saying that all of the products used were "natural," but that added coloring enhanced the appearance and preservatives kept the natural products "fresh." Of course, they didn't put this in big bold print. Instead, they buried the words at the bottom of the label next to an asterisk. The bold print now says "100% natural*."

0% SUPERNATURAL

There's a worldview that sees life as 100% natural, 0% supernatural. **Naturalism*** asserts that the physical world we experience around us is the only reality that can be known. To discover any truth, we must depend on observation and experimentation, which often means a full reliance on science. Many naturalists believe that whatever we discover through science is fact and therefore true. Anything we can't prove through science is not fact and therefore suspect. The word *natural* stands in opposition to *supernatural.* Naturalists believe that anything we can't test and prove through observation and experimentation would be supernatural, and that nothing supernatural exists. Or it belongs to the realm of faith, which for the naturalist indicates highly irrational personal belief.

For example, if your friend who is sick with cancer suddenly recovers, a Christian might think God supernaturally intervened. A naturalist will point you to the medicines or the doctors or something that can be explained scientifically as the cure. Even if an event cannot be fully understood scientifically, a naturalist will still insist that there is a scientific explanation for any apparently supernatural event. We may just not have the technology to detect the answers yet. Naturalists believe that when we attribute an event to a supernatural influence (such as God or the Devil), we're giving up on the chance to find the event's real cause(s). This insistence on a search for natural causes has led in the past to important breakthroughs, such as the discovery of bacteria that cause disease.

Materialism* is similar to naturalism. The distinction depends on deep philosophical arguments, but materialists agree with naturalists that the things we experience in the world around us are real and not illusions. One key difference between the two is that many materialists argue that every claim of truth must first be proven mathematically with priority given to physics.[1] Matter and energy—as defined by physics—exist. Nothing that isn't made of matter or energy (such as God or angels) exists.

You can think of it like this: Everything that we know in the universe has specific properties. Water is composed of hydrogen and oxygen. Even though we don't see the hydrogen or the oxygen, we can experience the physical results when we swim in the ocean or take a bath. Materialists calculate how water shaped something like the Grand Canyon by calculating the physical properties of water as it comes into contact with the physical properties of stone. A mathematical formula can be applied and a theory can be formulated about how long it took for the Colorado River to cut through all those layers of stone.

For naturalists and materialists, the emphasis is on the natural world and the truths waiting to be discovered through math or science. These truths will help every person cope with the experiences of life. Not all materialists or naturalists reject God, but the logic of this worldview tends to restrict God to a small corner of life and to place the most faith, for practical purposes, in science.

Because naturalists and materialists start without a concept of God as Creator of the universe, there is no need to describe the world in terms of a God. If God either doesn't exist or is largely irrelevant, then humans don't really need a relationship with God. Instead, humans exist as part of a cosmic process that led us to this moment in history. By using human reason and science, we can discover how the process has developed in the past and gain insight about where it could be going in the future.

PROGRESS AND REDUCTIONISM

Naturalism and materialism are two of the more powerful worldviews in our day. You will hear echoes of them over and over if you study science, medicine, law, history, or even education. While seldom stated overtly, this philosophy rests just under the surface in much of American life. Through science and technology, many believe we are evolving into a better society and world.

Certainly, naturalistic and materialistic worldviews have led to many significant discoveries in areas such as the medical field. Recent history has seen new treatments for patients suffering from a variety of diseases and ailments. Most of these innovations come from scientific research and development. Naturalists have also brought us much of the rapid rise in our material standard of living over the past two hundred years.

But because naturalists and materialists tend to be most interested in raising the material standard of living—physical health and comfort—they can undervalue other aspects of human life. For materialists, all of human life can be reduced to biological processes. Biology can be reduced to chemistry, and chemistry to physics. Can humans who hope, fear, love, and create be reduced to electrons and protons? From a purely naturalistic point of view, they can.

With reductionism—and a fascination with and dependence on technology—comes consumerism. Author Wendell Berry cautions: "Once the revolution . . . is under way, statesmanship and craftsmanship are gradually replaced by salesmanship—the craft of persuading people to buy what they do not need, and do not want, for more than it is worth."[2] Can humans be reduced to what we buy, drive, and wear?

WORLDVIEW SIGNPOSTS

God

It is difficult indeed for a naturalist to find any validity in a concept of God. Most would put all their eggs in the basket of human progress and science, leaving even the mention of God out of their conversations entirely. However, there are some naturalists who don't totally deny the existence of a God of some kind. One such philosopher was John Dewey.

Dewey embraced the idea of God, but to be consistent, he redefined what the term meant. The God of Christianity was a threat to Dewey's unity of humanity. He thought religion needed to be understood as a human experience. You could find the same experiences at a local club or organization that helped people. Dewey believed people experienced religion simply by working in unity with others. There was nothing special about a divine Being or human redemption. The more people deluded themselves to think in terms of an exclusive God, the more a group became a danger to the unity that everybody should share through the human experience of the natural world.[3]

Naturalists can tolerate a God who operates purely in the realm of "faith," who helps people get along and feel good about themselves. But a Creator who meddles in the universe, in the realm of space and time, can't exist.

Humanity

Naturalism holds that the explanation for the origins of human life rests solely on the shoulders of Darwinian evolution (on Darwinism, see page 131). Humans are no different from any other animal, and our presence here is the result of chance and change.

What has historically been called the human "soul" or "spirit" or "mind" is no more than a complex interaction of chemicals and electrical impulses in the brain. Love is a biochemical response. When the human brain dies, the person ceases to exist. Arguably, a human with enough brain damage to permanently lose self-awareness is a living body but no longer a person.

Furthermore, because we are animals, it's normal and healthy for us to have our natural drives and desires met. If we're hungry and food is available, we eat. If we want sex and a partner is available, we have sex. If our species were designed to be monogamous, we would instinctively stick to one partner — the fact that we don't shows we're not built that way. Our discussion on "The Sexual Revolution" (page 142) will address in more detail how naturalism affects sexual ethics.

Salvation

A savior for the human soul is unnecessary in the naturalist worldview. We don't need forgiveness from a God, nor union with an Absolute. We are simply animals who live and then die. But while salvation in this sense is irrelevant, *progress* is much to be desired.

Christians build their lives around a story of how God made humans, humans rejected God, God sought and eventually redeemed them through the work of Christ, and Christ will eventually return to bring his work to its fullness. Naturalists build their lives around a story of how humans evolved from other primates, humans progressed on their own from primitive to modern civilization, and humans will continue to progress until disease is conquered and human life is healthy and happy. One version of the naturalist story has humans spreading across the galaxy to other planets. Human mistakes (such as nuclear holocaust or environmental destruction) could derail this progress, but science can prevent this if we use it wisely. Essential to this story is a belief that humans are basically rational. Given increasingly powerful technologies, humans as a group will tend to make wise decisions about how to use them. Naturalists with less faith in human wisdom tend to be pessimistic about the future of our species and our planet.

Human beings can progress by embracing scientific development and by education. Naturalists support the removal of any mention of religion from the educational process, unless it's discussed as a phenomenon of social science (comparing cultures and their religions). Religion can't be proved by the methods of science, so its inclusion in education is regress, not progress.

Authority

Naturalists believe that human reason and other abilities (such as the ability to understand science and math) are the most trustworthy authorities. To derive your authority from a collection of ancient documents, such as the Bible, is foolhardy and perhaps even dangerous. Pure naturalism declares not just that science and math reveal some truth, but that they reveal all the truth worth knowing. Over time, through research and experimentation, the truth emerges clearly and unambiguously. (This is an absolute statement of pure naturalism. Many naturalists today, impressed by the unpredictable behavior of subatomic particles, refrain from such strong claims about knowing the truth.)

Naturalism's claim to truth rests on science and math, which in many cases are trustworthy. We know that $2+2=4$ and that the earth revolves around the sun. These are facts. In the sciences and advanced mathematics, all work is based upon human ideas and theories. These theories may be very good and best explain the data that scientists or mathematicians can observe. They may even be correct, just as $2+2=4$. But until they are conclusively proved, these theories are just suggestions that explain the facts.

Some theories stand up when tested in the lab or proved in a mathematical problem over and over again. These theories become the foundation for new work and research into other areas. Scientists and mathematicians take these theories that have a more solid basis and create what is known as a paradigm.

A paradigm is like a worldview for a set of facts. It explains all of the known data in the best possible way. The paradigm that can explain the known facts better than any other system becomes the dominant paradigm. Paradigms aren't static, however. They have to adjust to new information on a regular basis, because we continually discover new facts.

Sometimes these new discoveries challenge the dominant paradigm until it's no longer able to explain all of the facts. Then the paradigm must either be shifted to accommodate the new facts or replaced by a new one that better explains all of the data.

An excellent example of this process is the medieval view that the sun revolved around the earth. It's easy to understand why someone without a telescope or other means of studying the stars could reach this conclusion. After all, if you watch a sunset or even stay up all night for months, this is what appears to happen, right? The stars, moon, and sun appear to move and the earth appears to stand still.

A scientist named Copernicus had trouble with this view, however. The more accurately he and others charted the movement of the stars and planets night after night, the more complicated the data became with an earth-centered paradigm. He decided that the paradigm didn't adequately explain the data he observed. He set out to prove a sun-centered view of the solar system. In his paradigm, the earth rotated on an axis while it circled around a sun that didn't move.

Of course, we know this to be absolutely certain today. All of our data, including pictures of the earth from space, confirm that the earth really does revolve around the sun. Mathematically and scientifically, these facts have been verified over and over again. A paradigm had to shift from an old model to a new one.

Science has many paradigms with various levels of acceptance in the scientific community. One such paradigm that we will talk about in the next chapter is Darwinian evolution, which attempts to explain the origin of humanity. For naturalists and materialists who believe that everything must be explained through science, a challenge arises when new data bump into an accepted paradigm. Either their understanding about a subject must change to accommodate the new paradigm, or they cling to the old models in spite of crumbling support. The history of science is full of scientists who raged against new views.

Time

Most naturalists believe that nothing exists beyond life in this physical world. Concepts such as an afterlife, heaven, or hell simply don't fit in this worldview. We were born because of a process that developed millions of years ago. We will live on this earth and one day die. Then our bodies will return to dust and fertilize the ground for the next generation. The only thing that naturalists consider to be eternal is *matter*—the stuff out of which we and everything in the world are made. And astronomers and physicists have considerable evidence that the universe itself is in a long, slow process of burnout.

Jesus

Materialists and naturalists see no problem in affirming the historical Jesus who lived and died. He was a good teacher who helped people understand life and love, but that's it. Any mention of supernatural events (the virgin birth and Jesus' miracles, such as healing a blind man) is quickly dismissed as impossible, for it isn't verifiable.

NATURALISM AND CHRISTIANITY

It is abundantly clear that naturalism and Christianity differ on key points. For Christians, there is basically a trickle-down effect here. A Christian holds the Bible as the ultimate authority in life and the basis for truth in living. Everything else trickles down from there: a specific belief in God, Jesus Christ, miracles, the Resurrection, humanity's origin and purpose, and so on. Christians hold these views by faith, but they don't see faith as automatically opposed to reason and evidence. They think belief in the Resurrection, for example, is the best interpretation of the available historical evidence, because they think the biblical documents are essentially reliable.

Naturalism, on the other hand, views the Bible as a collection of documents full of superstitions and folklore. According to the dictates of science, they say there is no way that the Bible can stand as a verifiable and reasonable document.

There is a strand of Christianity that believes science to be dangerous and tries to avoid any connection with the scientific world at all costs. However, most Christians believe we can learn much from science. They also agree that human reason plays a vital role in our lives as beings created in the image of God. There are a number of Bible-believing scientists and researchers who claim that it's entirely reasonable to have faith in the Creator God, in his intentions for his creation, and in his Son, Jesus Christ. These scientists treat science as *a* source of truth and not *the* source of truth.

Christianity argues that faith lies at the base of every worldview, including naturalism. Christians would say that naturalists place just as much faith in science and reason as they place in the Bible. While some naturalists could affirm this idea, most reject the concept that naturalists hold to anything not reflected in actual reality.

NATURALISM AND MATERIALISM GLOSSARY

Materialism — The belief that the world we experience around us is composed of matter or material that can be proven through the exercise of physics.

Naturalism — The belief that everything in the world is the direct result of natural processes set in motion at some time in the past. Science gives us the keys to unlocking the mysteries of nature.

Darwinism

The waves lapped gently against the side of HMS *Beagle* while the sails flapped in the breeze. A man sat with his back to the rail of the ship's deck, writing feverishly in a large notebook. There had been so much to see over the last five years. His cabin was filled with journals of every shape and size chronicling the amazing animals and habitats he'd witnessed. Each volume painted an image of a world never before categorized in scientific literature. A recent graduate from the University of Cambridge, young Charles Darwin relished every discovery he made, yet he struggled with the question of how to explain the large diversity he found among the species he catalogued.

Once he returned to England, Darwin began to think through some of the larger issues. Although raised in the church, he struggled with the reliability of miracle accounts and the teachings of Jesus. This struggle eventually led him, at age forty-one, to proclaim himself an agnostic. The publication of his famous *On the Origin of the Species By Means of Natural Selection* soon followed.

Darwin's theory, commonly referred to as naturalistic evolution, accounts for man and all forms of life without a Creator God. All that life needed was a combination of atoms, movement, time, and chance. According to naturalism, our entire world is the result of random combinations of atoms. At later stages in this process, Darwinian **natural selection*** is at work.

Each species on the planet has one purpose: to reproduce itself. During the process of reproduction, occasional variants appear. If those variants are positive, more of the offspring with those variants survive, while fewer of those without the variant make it. Nature produces more offspring of each species than can survive, and because necessities are scarce, the offspring compete. Only the best and strongest—both within a species and between different species—will survive. We call this result "the survival of the fittest."

In this understanding, a vast period of time was necessary to produce the results we see today. At some point in a long process of natural selection, man arrived on the scene. The great complexity of human beings is not the result of a plan or a Creator. The species *Homo sapiens* was fit. So we survived.

As Darwinism came to be understood, all life-forms evolved from lower forms to more complex ones. The movement from simple to complex continues in the world around us, even though we may not always observe it. More recently, some evolutionary scientists have thrown out the neat progression of "lower" to "higher." Who is to say that humans are higher than cockroaches? Roaches have been successful survivors for much longer and over a wider variation of climates. If the name of the game is reproduction, not complexity, roaches rule.

RESPONSES TO DARWIN

For the purposes of this book, we're not primarily interested in whether Darwin's science is right or wrong. We're interested in understanding the worldview—Darwin*ism*—that his scientific theory has spawned.

The view that only time, chance, and processes such as natural selection have produced humans is called naturalistic evolution. It is part of the broader worldview of naturalism discussed above (page 119), and it gives no role of any sort to God.

Other understandings of evolution do make room for God. For example, one view is called **theistic evolution***. The thought here is that God created the universe and planet Earth in a very direct way, but he has worked from within earth's physical properties through evolution ever since. However, at some point along the way, God intervened with a direct creative act, instilling a living creature with a soul. This was how humans entered the scene. God created man by endowing one of the higher primates with a soul; he did not create man afresh as a completely new creature.

Another strand of thought is called **progressive creationism***. Although it may sound like theistic evolution, there are some differences. According to this view, God created afresh at several points separated in time. He did not make use of existing life at those points, merely modifying it. These were entirely new creations. Between these special moments of creation, God used channels of evolution to make creation develop. Of special significance here was the creation of man at one of these special moments. Man was not created out of some lower creature, but rather from the dust of the ground and the breath of God, as the biblical record states.

A more recent entry into the discussion of the origins of life is a movement called Intelligent Design, or ID for short. ID scientists directly challenge Darwinian evolution. They question whether time and chance alone could really create all we see around us. They believe there had to be some external intelligent force involved in this process. They note that even naturalistic physicist Max Tegmark observes that the universe appears to be "fine tuned for life." While Tegmark doesn't name God as the one who did the tuning, he does seem to open the door to an external creative force.[1] Because ID has made some inroads in public education, some people from the scientific community denounce it outright, seeing it as a veiled attempt to get God into the classroom. At the same time, some Christians are uncomfortable with a vague "intelligence" that may not equal the personal God of the Bible.

SOCIAL DARWINISM

Darwin wasn't the first European to theorize that humans had evolved from more primitive to more advanced states. He gathered data and suggested mechanisms by which evolution might have occurred from simpler to more complex species. But the idea that some humans (such as Africans) were less evolved than others (such as Europeans) was in the air in the colonially minded nineteenth century.

Darwin insisted that his ideas applied only to the biological realm, but others wanted to apply them to other areas of human development. Herbert Spencer's name is most commonly associated with this ripple effect from Darwin's thought. For Spencer, evolution became an umbrella philosophy for the development and growth of the whole of society. Spencer thought the unrestricted competition of early industrial capitalism was good for the human species, because the fittest would flourish while the weak would deservedly die young. This initial ripple proved unrealistic, but the next one was disastrous.

Adolf Hitler took the basis of Spencer's teachings and used it to justify the killing of millions of Jews during the Holocaust. Hitler viewed the Jews, as well as any race other than whites, as lower life-forms on the evolutionary scale. These *unfit* races were competing with the white race for the necessities of nature; therefore, exterminating them would be aiding society in achieving the highest goals of evolution.

Let's turn now and see how Darwinism intersects with our worldview signposts.

WORLDVIEW SIGNPOSTS

God

Although Darwin never fully embraced atheism, he did question the necessity of believing in God. In his *Origin of Species*, he dismissed the *need* for God as a Creator. Everything that's anything has come into being as a result of time and chance, not because God planned it that way.

Most who hold to Darwinian evolution today would deny that the God of Christianity exists. They fall in line with most naturalists and materialists in believing that supernatural occurrences or beings just do not exist. Theistic evolutionists and progressive creationists both agree to the need for God as a Creator, but they differ on the level and modes of involvement that God chose.

Humanity

Darwinism states that human beings simply appeared through the process of evolution and will continue to evolve until they die out or the planet ceases to exist. Any human ethics or morality also evolves constantly, along with the species. Therefore, labels such as "good" or "bad" aren't permanent. We could talk about what is good or bad for the species as a whole, for a particular culture, or for the survival of an individual's genetic code into the next generation. But that's quite different from a standard of "good" measured by the goodness of a God who transcends culture and who created our species.

Further, many cultural rules about what is good or bad fly in the face of our nature as animals. For instance, while it may seem good to the leaders of a culture to regulate sexuality, and thus control reproduction for their own ends, the human sex drive is really no different from any animal's sex drive. People's desires just *are*, like an animal's desires.

Salvation
Salvation would not be a term found in the vocabulary of most Darwinians. Any "saving" of society would happen through channels such as education and self-improvement. As human beings further develop in these areas, society and humanity will continue to move up the evolutionary scale.

Authority
As with other naturalist worldviews, the authority for Darwinist thinking is science and physics. Author David Quammen summarizes the response Darwinians give to those who question science's authority:

> Evolution by natural selection, the central concept of the life's work of Charles Darwin, is a theory. . . . If you are skeptical by nature, unfamiliar with the terminology of science, and unaware of the overwhelming evidence, you might even be tempted to say that it's "just" a theory. In the same sense, relativity as described by Albert Einstein is "just" a theory. The notion that Earth orbits around the sun rather than vice versa, offered by Copernicus in 1543, is a theory. Continental drift is a theory. The existence, structure, and dynamics of atoms? Atomic theory. Even electricity is a theoretical construct, involving electrons, which are tiny units of charged mass that no one has ever seen. Each of these theories is an explanation that has been confirmed to such a degree, by observation and experiment, that knowledgeable experts

accept it as fact. That's what scientists mean when they talk about a theory: not a dreamy and unreliable speculation, but an explanatory statement that fits the evidence. They embrace such an explanation confidently but provisionally — taking it as their best available view of reality, at least until some severely conflicting data or some better explanation might come along.[2]

Any stance from religious groups as to divine authority over or against human theory is met with the response, "Okay. Prove it." That is, prove it with the tools and methods of science and mathematics.

Time

The issue of time is a significant point of contrast between many religions and evolutionary thought. One of the foundation stones of evolution is that the universe is very old. This has to be the case for the many gradual developments of evolution to occur. Furthermore, evolution continues in the world around us, whether we see it occurring or not.

Religions such as Christianity and Islam hold that time will have a definite ending point. God will reveal himself to the world in some grand cosmic event, thereby closing the door on time as we know it. In an evolutionary understanding of the universe, time marches on for an eternity (or ends when the universe dies by natural processes already underway).

Jesus

As with God, Darwinists dismiss the Jesus of Scripture entirely. There might be a nod to him historically as a teacher in the Middle East during a particular period of time, but that is all.

It would be a moot point for someone to claim to be the Son of God, for there is no God.

DARWINISM AND CHRISTIANITY

While Darwin gave up on the *necessity* of God, some Christians have not given up on the *possibility* of Darwin's thought being a part of their worldview. Some conservative Christian theologians and scientists hold to theistic evolution, but the question always remains, "How does this view of God accord with the biblical data?" Some Christians see an obvious conflict between evolution and Genesis 1; others don't. The debate among Christians on this matter is grounded partly in science and partly in different views on what it means to say that the early chapters of Genesis are authoritative, literal, and "inerrant."[3]

Still, while Christians debate how to interpret the Bible, they agree that the Bible is the ultimate authority on the origins of the universe and human life. Therein lies a fundamental gap between Christians and Darwinists—authority. Darwinist thought views science as the only true authority. There is no way the Bible could be an authoritative book because it contains stories of miracles and the supernatural, which are not true. The Christian position is that miracles are by definition rare events that can't be repeated in a scientific study. To some extent, miracles and the supernatural can be evaluated with the methods historians and forensic investigators use to decide what probably happened in a historical event or a crime scene (What do the eyewitnesses say? Is there any evidence that the event was faked?). But if a miraculous or supernatural explanation for an event is automatically ruled out because of naturalist assumptions, no matter what the evidence, then Christians challenge those assumptions. And if there is insufficient evidence to prove or disprove an event that occurred two thousand years ago, naturalism says that to believe it is childish naiveté, while Christianity responds that *faith* can rest on something other than hard scientific proof.

Christianity has always regarded human beings as the pinnacle of God's creative work. The best responses to this belief have led to the viewpoint that God has entrusted humanity with this planet and everything it contains. Thus *stewardship*, *care*, and *responsibility* define a Christian's relationship to the earth and its creatures. The words "Christian" and "environmentalist" need not be mutually exclusive, as caring for the planet need not equal worshiping it. Sadly, some Christians have viewed humanity's status solely as one of privilege, and they have accepted abuse of land, resources, and other species. Much blood has been spilled beneath the banner of God. In a strange irony, this supposed Christian view sees humans—and often particular races or nations of humans—as the "fittest" and everything else in creation as "less than."

Darwinism's view of humanity is markedly different. We are just like the animals, no better and no worse. Anything that might distinguish us from the animals, such as a soul, would have to come from something like a god, which doesn't exist. Darwinists agree about this belief, but they don't all come to the same conclusions about how humans should relate to the nonhuman world.

For example, on the one hand, if we are simply one animal species among many, then animals should have the same legal rights as humans. To set protections on human life while allowing people to kill and eat animals offends some Darwinists. On the other hand, the idea of "the survival of the fittest" can be used to justify whatever humans might want to do in competing with other species for survival. Rather than conserving resources, we are all in competition for the resources on this planet, so we can resort to any means possible to get ahead and claim those resources. While some might label this behavior as bad, actually it's not, because morals and ethics are constantly evolving, so "good" and "bad" are incredibly fluid terms. In short, Darwinists debate the moral implications of their view of humanity, just as Christians do.

The Darwinist belief that humans are mere animals without immortal souls or a transcendent spiritual dimension has influenced modern life in many ways. But perhaps no effect has been more dramatic and more hotly contested than Darwinism's effect on views about sexuality. If we are mere animals, then following our instincts is the appropriate way to live. Rather than committing to just one spouse in this life (the Christian view), we should be free to follow animal instincts and have sexual relations with as many partners as we choose. If the name of the game is reproduction, then more offspring enhances humanity's chances of evolutionary development and survival.

Because this issue of sexuality has so many implications for the way we lead our lives, we will explore it more fully in the next section.

DARWINISM GLOSSARY

Natural Selection—One of the key mechanisms by which species evolve, according to Darwin. Genetic variations occur whenever a species reproduces, and those offspring whose variations make them best able to survive then live long enough to reproduce. In this way, nature "selects" the variations that survive through the generations.

Progressive Creationism—Similar to theistic evolution, but differs in that God did indeed create afresh at certain points in time. He used channels of evolution between these special moments.

Theistic Evolution—The belief that God created the world directly at the outset. However, from that point on he made use of evolutionary progress.

The Sexual Revolution

In the fields outside Bethel, New York, the crowd pulsed with the beat. The music of Jimi Hendrix, Janis Joplin, and Jefferson Airplane highlighted the 1969 Woodstock Festival. Billed as the largest rock-and-roll concert of all time, the event drew 450,000 people for a weekend of music. In the process, the underground hippie movement moved into the mainstream. It represented the full hedonism of the sixties and the coming of age of the sexual revolution.

All across America the cry was for "free love." People threw off the shackles of the traditional taboos imposed on sex. No longer did anyone have to worry about sex with entanglements. Many people justified their involvement in the sexual revolution by saying sex "was only natural." In other words, because sex is a natural function, we should have full freedom to engage our normal inclinations and drives.

The worldview behind these ideas is naturalistic and Darwinist. If, as Darwin suggested, we still possess our animalistic or primitive desires that need to be met, then why shouldn't we simply do what is natural? In addition, naturalism argues that religion, faith systems, and traditional morals are all part of our less-evolved human past. As people continue to advance, we will eventually abandon all religions as relics or superstitions of the past.

SEX BEFORE WOODSTOCK

The ideas of the sexual revolution of the 1960s can be traced back not just to Darwin, but to Sigmund Freud, who regarded sexuality as the basic framework of humanity. Freud saw human personality on three levels: (1) the *id*, which has desires and drives devoid of any morals, (2) the *ego*, or the conscious part of the personality, and (3) the *superego*, which regulates the id's drives and emotions. The supreme source of energy in the human is the *libido*, or sex drive, and all behavior is a modification or direction of this sexual energy.

According to Freud, society seeks to impose limits on the id and its gratification, but serious problems can result from this censorship. Although many of Freud's theories are no longer wholly accepted by most psychologists today, his basic tenets paved the way for the free love movement of the 1960s. This is naturalism taken one step further; humans are not just animals, but *sexual* animals, and sex is the most significant human experience. Whatever our sexual instincts—for one partner or many, same gender or opposite gender—if we are born with them, they are natural, and we harm ourselves psychologically if we place limits around their expression.

Let's look at our worldview signposts and see how these thoughts compare with Christianity.

WORLDVIEW SIGNPOSTS

God

Some deny God outright, but many soldiers in the sexual revolution claim a definite belief in God. In fact, many of the discussions today around sexual roles and behavior take place within the church and among Christians.

Humanity

The sexual revolution assumes that humans are merely or mainly animals. There is nothing intrinsically special about humans. Some advocates would say that what we do with our bodies doesn't affect our souls, because we don't have souls. Others would say that the "soul" is a name for the human personality, and the personality is healthier if sexual desires are openly expressed.

The sexual revolution strongly emphasizes the role of sex in our lives, elevating it to perhaps the most significant experience a human being can have. To deny ourselves of this experience with as many people and as many times as we can would be to deny our very humanity.

Salvation

Salvation for those in the sexual revolution of the 1960s was seen as the throwing off of traditional taboos and moral relics of the past, in particular those associated with religion. The human race would continue to evolve to higher levels of existence as more and more of these limitations were overcome. As each individual became freer, society would be liberated as well. The end result would be a utopia where we would all live together in harmony.

Authority

The slogan "If it feels good, do it" reveals the source of authority in the sexual revolution: the self. Each of us sets his or her own rules for conduct, especially when it comes to sexual behaviors. While Christians look to the Bible for authority on how we should live as sexual persons, naturalists see the Bible as hindering our development as human beings.

Time

The sexual revolution encourages people to have a good time while they can. The ancient Epicurean philosophy of "eat, drink, and be merry, for tomorrow we die" echoes the naturalist view that there is only this life and then the end.

Jesus

Many in the sexual revolution of the 1960s saw Jesus as a true revolutionary, dismantling threadbare religion and corrupt authority. Unfortunately, when the Jesus of the revolution was measured against the Jesus of the Bible, there was a disconnect. His popularity waned when the words of the biblical Jesus about sexuality proved too restrictive.

THE SEXUAL REVOLUTION AND CHRISTIANITY

The Bible portrays sex as a powerful and originally positive force that humans often abuse, with tragic results. The Song of Solomon celebrates monogamous love with graphic poetry. The story of Adam and Eve in Genesis 3 gives no indication that the first sin involved sex. Rather, the first sin involved a desire to be like God and run one's own life. The story says that relationship problems were a result, rather than a cause, of the first sin.

But the biblical writers are equally graphic in telling stories about what happens when human self-centeredness infects sexuality. Rape, incest, adultery, harems full of hundreds of wives and concubines, jealousy, competition for attention, obsession with one's appearance, the murder of a rival—it's all there.

From the biblical point of view, animals retain the sexual instincts that they were created to have, but virtually all human instincts have been tainted by sin. Just as some humans will overeat to a life-threatening extent, and some humans crave power or enjoy inflicting pain, so a person's hunger for sex is not necessarily a trustworthy gauge of his need for it. Furthermore, the Bible says that everything we do with our bodies affects the eternal part of us and the eternal part of the other person. Human sexuality is a meeting not just of bodies, but also of souls that can love or be numbed against love.

Yet as powerful and potentially beautiful as sex is, the biblical writers didn't see it as the most important experience of human life. They were far more interested in worshiping God, getting everybody fed and clothed, protecting people from violence, and having nonsexual relationships with other people. They would be dismayed by what they would see as our society's inordinate preoccupation with sex. The Christian writer C. S. Lewis commented:

> You can get a large audience together for a strip-tease act — that is, to watch a girl undress on the stage. Now suppose you came to a country where you could fill a theatre by simply bringing a covered plate on the stage and then slowly lifting the cover so as to let every one see, just before the lights went out, that it contained a mutton chop or a bit of bacon, would you not think that in that country something had gone wrong with the appetite for food? And would not anyone who had grown up in a different world think there was something equally queer about the state of the sex instinct among us?[1]

In all fairness, Christianity has not always known what to do with human sexuality. Many who looked to the church during the sexual revolution found nothing but fearful, pious rhetoric instead of incarnational truth. In combating the belief that we are just animals, some Christians gave the impression that we should focus only on our spirituality and try to overcome our physicalness. Yet the Bible portrays humans as beings who are equal parts mind, soul, and body, and to promote the first two at the expense of the third is always treading on thin ice.

Christianity holds that the sexual act is an incredibly powerful moment between two people of the opposite sex in a marital relationship; in it the two become one (Genesis 2:24). There has never been, nor ever will there ever be, anything *safe* about sex, so God set boundaries to keep this force in check. Within those boundaries, sex is something to not only be cherished, but enjoyed. Far beyond just skin on skin, there is something that takes place in those times on the level of *soul*. To take an opposite approach to our sexuality harms both us and those around us (1 Corinthians 6).

The issue of time deserves one final note. Those in the sexual revolution embraced the "eat, drink, and be merry, for tomorrow we die" mentality; today is all there is, so live life to the fullest. The Bible encourages Christians to live fully awake to the present moment and what is going on around us. There are many Christians who live entirely in some gilded age of the past or entirely in the future; this is not what the Bible teaches. Christianity embraces the afterlife — the hope of heaven — and that belief informs behaviors and attitudes today. Christians live with the understanding voiced by Maximus in Ridley Scott's *Gladiator*: "What we do today echoes in eternity."

Secular Humanist Worldviews

Secularism
Humanism
Individualism

*God, if there is a God, is irrelevant to
daily life.*

Secularism

What do you think of when you hear the word *secular*? The dictionary defines the word as "things that are not regarded as religious, spiritual, or sacred."[1] You may have heard people say things like, "I don't listen to secular music anymore; I only like Christian music," or, "She quit working for the church and has a secular job now."

Secularism is a little different. Like other worldviews, secularism is a philosophy of life and not a static category. As a worldview, it assumes that truth is found outside traditional religious systems. For a secularist, whether or not there is a God doesn't matter. Any benefit religious beliefs may offer can be attained through human effort alone. Secularists believe people can solve the essential mysteries of life. They argue that science and knowledge are foundational to building a better society and life for everyone. Technology allows the human race to continue down the road of progress.

The worldview of secularism holds that as society grows more and more secular, there will be less and less room for the supernatural and magical, that is, the religious. We should welcome this growth, for it will enable society to move beyond the religious wars that have wreaked havoc on the planet for centuries.

The trail of this thought can be traced back to men such as Max Weber and Friedrich Nietzsche. Nietzsche seems to have been the first to realize that terms like "right" and "wrong" were fading from the common language. What was replacing them was something called *personal choice*.

UTILITARIANISM

A nineteenth-century philosopher by the name of George Holyoake was the first to use the term *secularism*. He thought it would be helpful for people who struggled with the teachings of Christianity to have an alternative system by which to live. Holyoake believed that God did not exist and agreed with many of the assumptions of **naturalism*** about the beginning of the world. He had concerns, however, with naturalism's dehumanization of people. In a naturalistic system, people were viewed as animals and human desires were unrestrained. Holyoake believed people still needed an ethical system to guide their lives. Enter the ethic of **utilitarianism***.

Utilitarianism proposes that we make decisions based upon the greatest good that can be attained for the greatest number of people. Classic utilitarianism defines this "greatest good" as happiness. Actions are judged right or wrong solely on the basis of consequences—has happiness been achieved for the greatest number of people? As you can imagine, this gets sticky sometimes, depending on what group of people you are referring to and how they define happiness.

Consider the following scenario: You are a member of a college athletic team. One of the assistant coaches begins bringing members of your team gifts, such as clothes, electronics, and jewelry. You are fully aware that these practices are against the university's policies. The other students on campus are not aware of what's going on, so what they don't know shouldn't hurt them. Your team is experiencing happiness because of the gifts coming your way. Should you accept the gifts? If so, what's the basis for your compliance? Are you hesitant for some reason? What might that reason(s) be?

You've probably been presented with "what would you do?" scenarios before, and you realize that sometimes the discussion can go on like a tiger chasing his tail. The example we just mentioned does give you an idea as to how the ethic of utilitarianism could come into play in your life. A utilitarian doesn't ask, "What's the rule?" He or she asks, "What are the consequences? Will the benefits outweigh the harm?" In extreme cases, a utilitarian says, "If a few people have to die in order to save thousands of lives, it's worth it."

As you can see, this type of thinking takes the hand of naturalism in regard to authority—you are your own authority on right and wrong. Moral principles, whether from a university's policy or from the Bible, are secondary to your own judgment. In a secular system, self, or personal choice, is the basis for all decisions.

Let's observe what happens when secularism as a worldview interacts with society at large.

SECULARISM AT WORK

For secularists, religion is irrational. Some adherents to this view have taken an active role in seeking to remove religion's influence from society at large. Several groups of secularists organized in the twentieth century. One you've probably heard of is the American Civil Liberties Union (**ACLU***). Founded by Roger Baldwin in 1920, the ACLU is a legal organization that provides attorneys and legal expertise in cases where civil rights are allegedly being violated. They defend individuals regardless of race, color, creed, or religion.

A few notable cases involving the ACLU are the "Scopes Monkey Trial" in 1925, permitting the teaching of evolution in schools; the James Joyce trial that lifted the ban on the selling of his book *Ulysses* in the United States; and a more recent, *Lee v. Weisman* in 1992, which deemed the reading of officially sanctioned prayers at graduation ceremonies to be unconstitutional.[2]

Secularists look at human history and see a long trail of harm done in the name of religion. They don't think Christianity is any worse than other religions, but as the dominant religion in the West, it has done the most harm in Western culture. Where Christians see missionaries doing good by taking the light of the gospel around the world, secularists see colonialists imposing Western culture and religion onto oppressed peoples. Where Christians see themselves standing up for moral principles, secularists see them trying to impose their beliefs and limit the rights of women, or of adults in consenting sexual relationships. If Christian teaching isn't true and Christian moral values aren't right for every human, then evangelism and moral campaigns are destructive, harmful acts.

SECULAR FAITH?

There was a brief but significant period during the 1960s when a secular theology flourished. The "death of God" theology was primarily an American phenomenon and is most often connected with the name Thomas J. J. Altizer. This theology proposed the death (doing away with) of the transcendent (high, holy) God by ceasing acts like worship and prayer. It encouraged the rebirth of an immanent (near to humans) God who could be found in secular activities, such as the civil rights movement. The result was to be a new secular Christianity, world-affirming in purpose, that sought to enjoy God rather than using or needing him.[3] As is the case with secularism, man was the standard. Insight or truth could be found here on earth through mankind. There is no God who speaks with truth through prophets or biblical authors.

WORLDVIEW SIGNPOSTS

God

The stance of secularism is that God is not necessary. Any concept of God would go hand in hand with religion, and society and mankind are better off leaving the constraints of religion behind. The spectrum of secularism includes **agnosticism*** and **atheism***. Some who hold those views believe that human beings invented God in order to construct a system of morals for people.

Humanity

Secularism is often tied to a concept called humanism. We will talk about this more in the next chapter, but we should note that humans have a fairly high position in this worldview. Naturalistic concepts of evolutionary development put humans into the place of God or gods, with the right to define what is right and true. According to secularist scientist Carl Sagan, "Men may not be the dreams of the gods, but rather that the gods are the dreams of men."[4] When freed from religion's brainwashing, humans are essentially good and rational. Through a democratic process, they will naturally make good decisions that will protect everyone's rights and create an increasingly happy society.

Salvation

Secularists argue that salvation for humanity can only come through evolution and human effort. Since people continue to believe the "myth" that God exists, progress toward the next stages of evolution is stalled. By eradicating theism and teaching "rational" ideas, secularists will help all people move forward into a time when we will no longer need rules. Instead, people will choose to do the right thing because they experience enlightenment through reason.

Authority

For most secularists, people create their own standards. They should be able to police themselves, make right decisions, and advance civilization. Secularists are often influenced by naturalism, so they often affirm that science presents an accurate view of the universe. In this way, science aids decision making. Through scientific discoveries, people can make good choices based on the knowledge gained.

A utilitarian ethic often drives the application of these scientific discoveries. If the cloning of human embryos, for example, shows promise of leading to cures for diseases, then that good consequence outweighs moral questions about cloning.

Time

Secularists take a long view of time. While humans are only on earth for a brief period, secularists believe that our current state of evolution has taken millennia to develop. Time is not controlled by an external force or God. Instead, humans have to comply with the seasons of nature. At some point in the evolutionary journey of humanity, we may be able to discover through science the means to live forever.

At death, secularists don't believe there is a literal heaven or hell. Instead, life simply ends. You succumb to the pattern that nature has laid before you. You were born through the natural process, and now your remains in the ground help continue that process.

Jesus

Since secularists deny that God exists, or at least believe that a person couldn't ever know him, asking any questions about Jesus would be a moot point. For secularists, Jesus was at best a good human being whom the disciples grossly misunderstood. The disciples created an aberrant form of Judaism that misrepresented Jesus and his teaching. Further, in previous centuries the church abused the name of Jesus to justify the atrocities and wars of religion. Secularists hope to remedy these errors through free thought.

SECULARISM AND CHRISTIANITY

For most Christians, it's easy to see the stark contrasts between secularism and the teachings of Scripture. Ideas such as the denial of God, a human-based authority structure, and an absolute trust in science stand in opposition to most Christians' worldview. These boundaries become harder to detect when secularism is merged with humanism, which we will talk about in the next chapter.

Secularists assume that human rationality or human thinking is superior to any type of revelation found in the Bible. Many secularists think of Christians or other theists as irrational or even dangerous, since they hold on to what many secularists call legends.

There are some Christians who believe that referring to our culture as "secular" is actually incorrect. Writers such as Lesslie Newbigin contend that what "has come into being is not a secular society but a pagan society, not a society devoid of public images but a society that worships gods which are not God."[5] Newbigin believes that Christians have uncritically accepted the "secular society" and its goals—freedom and tolerance among religions and worldviews. More will be said about this in the section on postmodernism.

As we continue our journey from secularism to humanism, we will discover that secularism and humanism have become great friends in the last century. Some of the claims of the secular worldview have even morphed into what is called secular humanism. All this is just around the corner.

SECULARISM GLOSSARY

ACLU—The American Civil Liberties Union. Founded by Roger Baldwin in 1920. The ACLU uses the legal system to defend its interpretation of the Constitution and individual rights contained therein.

Agnosticism—The belief that if God exists, we cannot know him.

Atheism—The belief that God does not exist.

Naturalism—The belief that people and the world we see around us are the result of time and chance.

Utilitarianism—A philosophical system that seeks to achieve the greatest good for the greatest number of people.

Humanism

THE ROOTS OF HUMANISM

Around five hundred years ago, a group of European scholars began studying ancient texts in the original languages. Their study helped reconnect them and others in Europe with the ancient world. Their thinking revitalized art, music, history, poetry, and other disciplines of the "humanities." They came to be known as humanists.

While the early humanists valued what they learned from the great ancient and medieval thinkers, they stressed that all humans have the capability to learn and understand essentials such as how the world works and what the Bible teaches. At that time (the 1400s and early 1500s), the church forbade laypeople to read Scripture or other sacred books for themselves. Church leaders believed that only priests or specially trained men could explain the Bible to ordinary people. Literacy was rare, and theological sophistication even rarer. The idea of a merchant or a blacksmith's wife deciding for himself or herself what the Bible meant seemed a recipe for disaster.

Humanists disagreed. They believed everyone could and should read any text, even the Bible, for herself. They were convinced that over time, people would escape spiritual darkness as the biblical text enlightened them. This concept revolutionized Europe, the church, and eventually all of Western society.

These early humanists stressed two things. First, all humans are capable of learning. Second, through education, social change can happen. And social change did happen. In 1517, Martin Luther nailed to the door of the Wittenberg Castle church a list of ninety-five serious problems he saw in the wider church. He unintentionally sparked a revolution that led thousands of Christians across northern Europe to break away from the Catholic Church headed in Rome. They came to be called Protestants and founded what eventually became new denominations.

Luther spurred the Protestant reforms in Germany, John Calvin led a formal change of the church in the Swiss city of Geneva, and Ulrich Zwingli changed the Swiss city of Zurich. From these locations, Protestant ideas spread throughout Europe like wildfire. Not coincidentally, each of the reformers translated the Bible into the language of their people so that ordinary individuals could read and interpret the Bible themselves.

The Roman Catholic hierarchy saw the reformers as destroyers of the unity and truth of the faith and tried to suppress them violently. Where the reformers could get a king or a prince on their side, the church responded in kind. Political power was intertwined with the right to interpret the faith. War, arrests, torture, and assassination ravaged Europe.

Because of this bloodshed, humanists began to stress another tenet in their worldview: religious toleration. After witnessing many battles between reformers and Catholics, or between one group of reformers and another, these early humanists concluded that freedom of religion was the only way to promote unity in the public arena. Catholics saw the cry for tolerance as the abandonment of truth and rightful authority. They were also concerned about maintaining their political power, just as Protestant princes were keen to wrest power for themselves. Humanists continued to argue for religious freedom.

THE FRUITS OF HUMANISM

Fast-forward to the twenty-first century. Humanism today, while embracing some of these early concepts, has morphed into a different belief system. No longer a reform movement within Christianity, modern humanism for the most part separates human beings from any concept of God. Like secularists, humanists believe people themselves, not God, are the key to unlocking the door of truth.

A phrase you have no doubt heard during your lifetime is secular humanism. The *Humanist Manifesto*[1] is the wedding of secularism and humanism in a nutshell. Now in its third version, the *Humanist Manifesto* declares:

1. The scientific method is the best way of increasing our knowledge. Through the use of observation, experimentation, and analysis, humans grow in their quest for truth and overall intelligence.

2. Naturalism must be assumed. Humans are just a part of nature and have evolved into our current place in nature.

3. Values are determined by human circumstances, human need, and human want. Through logic and rational thought, every person can make right decisions that allow for the freedom of every person.

4. Because humans are social creatures, everyone ought to create mutually beneficial relationships that are not violent—including relationships between countries. All wars could be avoided if relationships were established between all peoples.

5. Developing a global economy and community will lead to the happiness of everyone on the planet because resources could be openly shared and distributed to everyone.[2]

The document closes with a bold statement:

Humanists are concerned for the well being of all, are committed to diversity, and respect those of differing yet humane views. We work to uphold the equal enjoyment of human rights and civil liberties in an open, secular society and maintain it is a civic duty to participate in the democratic process and a planetary duty to protect nature's integrity, diversity, and beauty in a secure, sustainable manner.[3]

Humanism is a diffuse outlook rather than an organized institution, so not everyone who calls herself a humanist would fully embrace the *Humanist Manifesto*. However, the *Manifesto* expresses some ideas that are common among many humanists.

A RETURN TO THE ROOTS?

The term **religious humanism*** has gained prominence in recent years and deserves mention in this discussion. This term may be problematic for some people who have only heard the word *humanism* in the context of deeply secular, modern philosophies. But as noted earlier, humanism originated within a context of profound religious faith.

The term *religious humanism* suggests a tension between two opposed terms—heaven and earth. However, religious humanism sees this as a creative, not destructive, tension. One analogy for understanding this balance comes from the Christian doctrine of the Incarnation, which holds that Jesus was both human and divine. Religious humanists hold the paradoxical meeting of these two natures to be a model by which to understand the many dualities we experience in life: flesh and spirit, nature and grace, God and Caesar, faith and reason, justice and mercy.[4]

Religious humanists seek to live within this tension, balancing commitment to the historic truths of religion with openness to the world. They highly regard symbolism, imagery, and language, for they believe them to be crucial in forming attitudes as well as prejudices. Their work is tied to the literary and theological traditions of figures such as Augustine of Hippo, T. S. Eliot, and Flannery O'Connor.

WORLDVIEW SIGNPOSTS

God

Secular humanism seeks to elevate human abilities and rational thinking above any belief in God. While some secular humanists observe Christianity and other religions as interesting relics of the past, most believe that the religious are clinging to part of the prior evolution of human society. For society to move into the next level of social evolution, people need to abandon the hopeless view that God exists.

Humanity

Secular humanists sometimes quote a statement by the ancient Greek philosopher Protagoras: "Man is the measure of all things." That is, the individual human person, not "a god or an unchanging moral law, is the ultimate source of value."[5] People, not God, are the source of truth, the goal of life, and the solution to human problems.

The near-divine status of the individual is moderated by an insistence that we should be selfless toward others and respect human rights. Most humanists believe strongly in caring for all of humanity, not just oneself. Humanists are often active in helping others or advocating human rights.

But what regulates or motivates selflessness toward others? Humanists usually point to utilitarian ethics or simple altruism to explain why anyone should care for another. The high intrinsic value of every human person seems obvious to humanists. For secular humanists, it doesn't rest on an outside authority, such as the belief that God created humans in his image. It is simply a fact.

Salvation

When it comes to salvation, humanists would give a hearty nod to education. Any salvation, for the individual or for the group, comes by way of learning (focusing on the humanities—art, music, literature, poetry, the scientific method, and so forth). Learning presents the possibility, at least, of a beautiful and diverse society, built on the virtue of tolerance. Any notion that someone like Jesus was necessary for salvation would be dismissed. We, as humans, have the ability to achieve truth on our own.

Authority

As we have already mentioned, the basic authority of humanism is the individual. No external system of laws by a divine Being should even be contemplated. The laws we enact as humans through the process of government are in place to protect the weak and help people who don't have enough education to make the right choices. Eventually, as society evolves, everyone will be able to police himself and will always do the right thing.

Because humans are the ultimate authority for secular humanists, there is no set standard for right and wrong. Every standard of morality is simply self-imposed.

Time

Because you are the final authority, make the most of life while you can. This is the only time you have. Secular humanists vary on how they deal with the question of time. Some advocate living in the moment: Do anything and everything that makes you happy as long as you don't hurt others. Some believe you possess a unique opportunity to give back to society and help push it along until its next stage of evolution.

While Christianity and other religions encourage individuals to live with an awareness of the afterlife, such an idea is the antithesis of what modern humanists believe. Humans only participate in the ebb and flow of life here and now.

Jesus

Humanists would be hard-pressed to say that Jesus was anything other than a good man. Some would go so far as to say that he was a great example for all of humanity, but in the end, he was just a man. Christians say that Jesus was both a man and God incarnate, a man who was fully God and fully human. His death and resurrection profoundly shaped all of history. For humanists, this can only be a myth.

SECULAR HUMANISM AND CHRISTIANITY

Christian leaders have long seen secular humanism as an enemy of Christianity. The fear is that if secular humanists prevail, they will stifle religious liberty and shut Christians out of the public arena. Whether or not these fears are warranted is still unfolding. And in practice, relations between secular humanists and Christians range from conflict to adaptation.

On the conflict side, many humanists advocate a society that is free of values or morals that apply to everyone. They believe such a society will give diverse people the most liberty to live by the values they choose. Christians often respond that there is no such thing as a values-free or morals-neutral system. Every person has values and morals. Their worldview determines what those morals and values are. And if you want to get at the root of a moral system, discover its central authority. In the case of secular humanism, that authority lies in the individual. Ideally, that person acts with the best interests of others in mind, but the person still has the final say. So a theoretically morals-neutral system that leaves standards up to the individual is effectively a system run according to secular humanist values.

Of course, secular humanists express dismay at some of the values Christians actually live by. Christians don't always promote, live, and seek to reproduce truly biblical values and morals. Some secular humanists feel that in the Christian community, middle-class American values (such as achievement, upward mobility, and the pursuit of possessions) sometimes replace biblical ones.

This tendency to mesh Christianity with middle-class American values is an example of **syncretism***. Syncretism meshes two or more different belief systems together (we will talk more about syncretism later, beginning on page 193). And in fact, far from opposing secular humanism, many Christians mesh the biblical worldview with the secular humanist worldview. They don't always do this consciously, but rather adopt secular humanist beliefs and habits from the culture around them. They go to church and perhaps listen to Christian music, but as they go through a day at work or school, they live as though God doesn't exist, as though humans should make up their own minds about what's good or bad, and as though life is primarily about achieving their full potential as humans through achievement and success, measured in honors and dollars.

At its best, humanism places a high value on people — other people as well as oneself. But because it is often mingled with individualism, life often ends up being all about *me*. We'll look at individualism more deeply in the next chapter.

HUMANISM GLOSSARY

Religious Humanism—Religious humanists seek to live within the tension of commitment to the historic truths of religion with openness to the world.

Syncretism—Meshing more than one philosophy, religion, or worldview to form a new one. Syncretists often don't worry about whether the perspectives they are putting together are logically compatible or in conflict.

Individualism

In the chapter on humanism, we talked about how that world-view seeks the best in people and encourages individuals to act with someone else's interests in mind. This is called **altruism***. By following The Golden Rule—Do unto others as you would have them do unto you—society and relationships work better.

We must remember, however, that society and relationships are composed of individuals—individuals who have their own history, upbringing, and ideas. In an individualistic worldview, the focus is on each person and the power inside of us to make a difference. Yes, this sounds a lot like humanism. The two are related in some respects. But as we talk about individualism, we are going to discover that individualistic thought is conceived a bit differently.

At its core, individualism stresses the freedom and **autonomy*** of the individual. Self-reliance—making it on your own—is its core value. You should be able to dress yourself, drive a car, choose a career, choose where you live, and choose how you live. Nobody should limit these freedoms except in situations where your actions affect others. As the maxim goes, "My freedom to swing my fist ends where your face starts."

At the same time, you shouldn't expect society to take care of you. If you're disabled (or differently abled), you need opportunities to work and support yourself. If you're elderly, you should have planned for retirement so you won't have to depend on your children or society. To need others is to be a burden, and individualists dread the thought of being a burden to others.

Let's look at some history to help clarify where individualism comes from.

JUST BEING ME

Individualism is actually one of the themes of another philosophy: **existentialism***. The name most commonly associated with early existentialism is Søren Kierkegaard. Kierkegaard emphasized existence over essence. In other words, the question "Is it?" is more important than "What is it?" Existentialism is a multifaceted philosophy, encompassing several themes. For our purposes, let's look at how individualism springs from existentialism in two areas: individuality and freedom.

Any effort to fully define a person will fall short, so say the individualists. Categories such as male or female, American or Asian, blue-eyed or green-eyed, are feeble attempts when it comes to the "real" person who exists. Each of us is an individual who is supremely unique and as such should have the freedom to express that individuality to its fullest. Therefore, rather than accepting what the crowd or society may think or believe, you are to forge your own path. Ralph Waldo Emerson speaks clearly here:

> There are the voices which we hear in solitude, but they grow faint and inaudible as we enter into the world. Society everywhere is in conspiracy against the manhood of every one of its members. . . . The virtue in most request is conformity. Self-reliance is its aversion. . . . Whoso would be a man must be a nonconformist. . . . Nothing is at last sacred but the integrity of your own mind.[1]

The language may sound old-fashioned, but the thoughts are contemporary. The goal here is to be your own person, have your own thoughts, and do your own thing. This is seen as authenticity. Society is trying to squeeze you into its mold, and you should resist that—not in order to pattern yourself after some other mold, such as the way of thinking and living that Jesus modeled, but in order to do what you want to do.

If someone doesn't agree with your thoughts or actions, that person just doesn't understand you. He probably never fully can. Individual freedom, exempt from any concern with society, is the consistent drumbeat of individualism.

A LITTLE MORE ME

When taken to its logical extreme, this approach to life leaves no room for other people. If you only look out for yourself, how are you supposed to get along with other people in a group or in society as a whole? At its extreme end, individualism produces **anarchy***. Anarchy results when people rebel against authority structures and seek to rule their own lives. In a state of anarchy, anything you want to do is right. Theft, scandal, or even murder is an option if that is what you want to do.

You and I are part of larger social structures. Unless you decide never to leave your house, you will come face-to-face with the reality of how social structures work. There are limits on everything from how fast you can drive to how many terms an elected official can serve. You could try to do things your own way and refuse to obey the speed limit, but you will eventually have to pay the price. You could consistently miss work, but you should prepare to be fired and begin looking for other employment. You get the idea. Individualism in its radical forms doesn't work because, as

John Donne wrote in his famous *Meditation XVII*: "No man is an island, entire of itself."

It's rare to find this form of radical individualism. Instead, individualism tries to adapt itself to other perspectives. Secular humanism, for example, employs many elements of individualism. Even Christianity has unknowingly taken on elements of individualism. We will talk more about that later. For now, let's turn to the main points of an individualist worldview.

WORLDVIEW SIGNPOSTS

God

Little kids often assert their independence by claiming, "I can do it myself!" Those with an individualistic worldview live this phrase with regard to God. Many good people believe they can live without any divine assistance. Some even view God as a crutch for the weak. They believe that he cannot or will not intervene directly in the life of any person. For most individualists, God is distant if he exists at all.

Individualism doesn't necessarily deny God's existence. Some very strong Christians emphasize the role of the individual in the church. And even in the Bible, people respond to the gospel as individuals. No one can put faith in Christ for you. In addition, the church is formed by individuals who work together to accomplish the work God gave us to do. But biblical individualism relies on God's power and is balanced by biblical interdependence. The people of God are together God's family, Christ's body, the Holy Spirit's temple, a kingdom of priests. We are accountable to the Creator of the universe and to the family of believers for the actions we perform as individuals.

Humanity and Authority

As you might expect, individualists place a high value on the uniqueness of each person. Nothing should stand against your being, thinking, and doing what you want to do. Any obstacles of this kind must be overcome, for they are keeping you from being the person you really are. This stress on the autonomy of each person naturally leads to each of us being our own authority. There is no external authority, such as God, or any document that could guide us in our living, such as the Bible or Koran.

Individualists are highly suspicious of authority figures. History is full of examples when political leaders became dictators, religious leaders twisted the faith for their own ends, and parents abused children. Because power corrupts, individualists feel it's safer to give parents, teachers, and leaders as little power as possible.

Individualists especially don't trust any organized group, such as a church or a denomination, to say what the Bible (or some other religious document) means and how people should live. For Christian individualists, every individual is his own priest, free to interpret the Bible however he thinks best. While Martin Luther and other early Protestant reformers argued that the Bible belonged to the people as a community, rather than just to the leaders (see page 159), more-individualist Protestants feel that the Bible belongs to each individual believer.

Salvation

Individualists find salvation primarily through fame. Their question is, "Once your life is over, will people actually remember you for the things you did or said?" For many who accept individualism as a worldview, only fame or notoriety is eternal. This aspect of individualism is seen in the godlike status that many celebrities achieve in the public mind.

The Bible says grace is given freely to those who are willing to accept it, but individualism influences people to seek ways to somehow earn God's favor. Self-reliance seems more admirable than dependence. An individualist isn't comfortable with the Christian belief that no amount of work we could ever do can earn salvation.

Time

Human beings don't fare well against the perpetual ticking of the clock. We age, get wrinkles and gray hair, sag. Eventually, we die. Aging and death are two of the greatest challenges to individualism, because everyone faces the same fate and nothing can be done about it. Yet some try. A good example of this is the rise of cosmetic surgery. People take expensive and sometimes drastic steps to try to "turn back the clock." From Botox injections to tummy tucks, people shake a fistful of dollars in the face of time. Such thinking and living leads to a preoccupation with youthfulness and a sometimes overt discrimination against the older members of our society.

Jesus

Since individualism elevates each person as high as possible, there is no room for a Jesus who is King to be in charge. The idea that we have no rights that Jesus doesn't give us sounds totalitarian to individualists. Individualists hear the slogan "Jesus is Lord" and fear Christians mean, "This or that pastor who interprets the words of Jesus is Lord." Even if the individual retains the right to interpret the Bible for herself, it's still hard for her to submit to what she sees the Bible or Jesus saying, because that still limits her power as an individual.

Jesus gave freely of himself, but individualism tries to control personal destiny. Jesus told his followers to deny themselves; individualism tells people to assert themselves to get their own way. To the individualist, Jesus' words and actions seem like masochism. Here is one example, in which Jesus talks about why he is freely going to his death:

> The truth is, a kernel of wheat must be planted in the soil. Unless it dies it will be alone—a single seed. But its death will produce many new kernels—a plentiful harvest of new lives. Those who love their life in this world will lose it. Those who despise their life in this world will keep it for eternal life. All those who want to be my disciples must come and follow me, because my servants must be where I am. And if they follow me, the Father will honor them.[2]

INDIVIDUALISM AND CHRISTIANITY

Christianity and individualism conflict at various points. The Bible suggests that deep inside, each of us wants to believe we are the boss. The decision to trust Christ must be made by an individual, but when she places her faith in Christ, the Bible says she surrenders her rights to him. She is no longer her own.[3] She belongs to Christ and is interdependent with her fellow believers. Paul used the analogy of the human body to illustrate this point.[4]

The elements of our body all work together in harmony to keep us alive. Research into causes of cancer has discovered that some cancers are caused by elements in our bodily system attempting to do things on their own. These "free agents" begin to slowly shut the body down and eventually kill it. Christians believe that those in the church who stress their own importance or insist on the validity of individualism are bound to injure others and harm their relationships even if they don't intend to.

Christians use the word *community* a lot. For some it refers to gathering in a specific place at a certain time each week. For others it refers to informal gatherings with friends, and still others define it as time with people who share like interests. Jean Vanier, founder of the L'Arche Communities for the mentally handicapped, defines it like this:

> The difference between community and a group of friends is that in a community we verbalise our mutual belonging and bonding. We announce the goals and the spirit that unites us. We recognise together that we are responsible for one another. We recognise also that this bonding comes from God; it is a gift from God. It is he who has chosen us and called us together in a covenant of love and mutual caring. . . . Communities are truly communities when they are open to others, when they remain vulnerable and humble; when the members are growing in love, in compassion and in humility.[5]

In this view, when individualism creeps into community, the results are rivalry, competition, jealousy, and often hatred.

The phrase "It's all about me" is a mantra of our society. Some in Christian circles have taken the opposite-end-of-the-spectrum approach and declared, "It's not about me at all." To some, this appears to be the approach of the Bible and the standard by which Christians should live. For others, a middle-ground approach might be, "Sometimes it's about me, just not all the time."

INDIVIDUALISM GLOSSARY

Altruism—The belief that humans will give of themselves or their resources without thinking of themselves.

Anarchy—Extreme human rebellion against authority structures. Violence is always a by-product.

Autonomy—Freedom from any attachments or outside influence from any other person.

Existentialism—The belief that existence is more important than essence and man has absolute freedom of choice.

Postmodern Worldviews

Postmodernism
Syncretism
Pragmatism

But hey, that's okay for you, just not for me! It's pomo! Postmodern! Geez, you know, weird for the sake of weird.
—MOE SZYSLAK

Postmodernism

Take several apparently unrelated plotlines, crisscross them with each other, fill them with a group of seemingly regular people, and then watch them all come together into something resembling a whole. What do you have? Only one of the most successful television sitcoms in history: *Seinfeld*. One especially memorable episode was told backward, starting with the end of the story and working itself back to the beginning. Make sense? Maybe, maybe not; but a lot of people tuned in. The producers of this show were presenting one of the key elements of postmodern thought — loopy thinking. One thing doesn't necessarily have to lead to another as you might expect. It could lead to something entirely different and unexpected. The writers set out each week to **deconstruct*** the standard ideas about what a story line was supposed to look like and then recreate it.

THE TROUBLE WITH TRUTH

Postmodernism* began long before Jerry, George, Kramer, and Elaine came on the scene. The term may have first been used by Federico de Onis in 1930 but did not become a part of our vocabulary until it became associated with art and literature in the 1960s and architecture in the 1970s. The 1980s saw its meaning infused into the arts, politics, certain branches of science, and even theology.

To avoid confusion, let's go back in history a bit. Modernism was a movement that began back in the 1800s. Tied very closely to the naturalistic worldview, modernists believe the world is full of order and can be understood by anyone through observation — objectivity. We can categorize, label, and interpret the things in the world because it is filled with objective truths we can discover. The few things left in the world that defy explanation will eventually be understood or might possibly be ultimately unknowable. As you can see, modernism carries with it a level of *certainty*.

Out of this certainty there arises something called a **metanarrative***. A metanarrative is simply an overarching story that helps us explain life or any element of it, such as religion, politics, or what it means to be human. For example, evolution could be interpreted as a metanarrative because for those who believe in it, evolution explains human origins. It is a story that gives meaning and explanation based upon an interpretation of data. And it is very much a story: "Once upon a time there were single-celled organisms swimming around in primeval pools. As they reproduced, some of them had variations that helped them survive better than others. . . . And behold, some of the primates had offspring with larger brains, and their children's children's children stood up on their back legs, and after many long generations, a human was born. . . ."

According to postmodernism, we are moving *beyond* modernism — beyond the machine, beyond science as the end-all, beyond analysis as the approach to life, and beyond a belief in metanarratives. In fact, all metanarratives need to be deconstructed. We need to move beyond acceptance of these overarching explanations to an honest appraisal of truth. We have to admit that we're not nearly as certain as modernism would have us believe. "No metanarrative, it appears, is large enough and open enough genuinely to include the experiences and realities of all peoples."[1]

It will be helpful to understand a little of the basis of metanarratives. In short, they give explanations based on what are called **truth claims***. Truth claims are things that people believe. Postmodernism views truth in two ways:

1. *Objective truth.* Those who argue for objective truth assert that some truth can be known. Whether proved by science or otherwise, truth is truth. It is 1+1=2 and knowing that stealing is always wrong. Objective truths stand whether we believe them or not; they simply are true. Postmodernism denies objective truth exists in reality.

2. *Subjective truth.* If there are no objective standards or truths, truth can be whatever you make it. This is called subjective truth. It is true according to the viewer (*I* believe . . .). While mathematical certainty (such as 1+1=2) challenges ideas of subjective truth, those who argue for this perspective claim that stealing might not always be wrong. Postmodernism leans toward the idea that all truth is subjective.

WHATEVER WORKS FOR YOU

Instead of aiming for a new metanarrative or a universal worldview, postmodernism focuses on individual system-building. Whatever the individual views as truth is the only truth for that person. No single standard of truth exists. This idea is commonly called relativism. The absence of an organizing story line isolates each individual into a separate "truth universe." In other words, for postmodernism, truth is what you make it: "whatever works for you."

While postmodernism is seen in the lives of people of different generations, it has been noted that those with the strongest tendency toward postmodernism are people whom social scientists currently call Millennials. Social science doesn't claim to be exact, but for our purposes, the Millennial Generation comprises those children born between 1980 and 2001. Two important characteristics of postmodernism are common in this age group: a thirst for experience and a commitment to **tolerance***.

Experiential learning is the name of the game in postmodernism. Something must be experienced, and only then can an assessment be made. Doing in order to learn covers everything from video games to classroom instruction to spirituality. Remember, whatever the individual takes as truth is the only truth for that person. Therefore, postmodernists honor a wide berth of tolerance. Everyone should be able to discover his own truth (by way of experience) and then live out that truth (by way of personal freedom).

Some pose a question here: How can two opposite claims coexist side by side and both be true? Postmodernists respond by reminding people that truth is subjective. You have your important truths, and I have mine. If truth is not objective, we are simply *interpreters* of truth. Everyone can have their own perspective as long as they don't force it on others. In the realm of ideas, every perspective is valid and every opinion deserves to be heard and presented.

IT'S STILL EARLY

It needs to be stated that the early days of an emerging philosophy are usually quite critical of the worldview already in place. Thus, much of what we hear from some postmodern thinkers sounds critical of any kind of modernism. Postmodernism is still working out views and visions, and time will no doubt reveal inconsistencies and gaps in postmodernism, as it has with other worldviews. Some believe that postmodernism has already passed as a worldview. Some see it as just now coming into its own. One thing is for certain: This worldview permeates our culture. We'll continue to flesh it out as we look at our worldview signposts and three different aspects of postmodernism in the next few chapters.

WORLDVIEW SIGNPOSTS

God

With some exceptions, the deconstructed world has no place for a God who claims to be real for everybody and in charge of everything. Still, it's not uncommon for postmodernists to assert that some form of a divine Being does exist. In fact, the generations most influenced by postmodernism tend to be some of the more religious.[2] However, when postmodernists frame their religious beliefs, most stay outside the scope of any major religious tradition. They choose instead to define their faith for themselves. Why?

The reason goes back to the postmodern distrust of metanarratives. For the postmodernist, metanarratives mean power. All traditional religions, including Christianity, are simply instruments of power that try to force their own interpretation on others. This violates the postmodern belief in tolerance.

Postmodernists are particularly troubled by religions like Christianity and Islam that actively seek to win others over to their views. In the eyes of a postmodernist, to insist that Christ (or Allah) has an exclusive claim on every person's life, or to say that Christ is the only way to God, treads on the individual's autonomy to define her beliefs for herself.

Humanity

Postmodernism has a high view of humanity. You might have caught on to this earlier as we talked about the importance of the individual in this system. According to the teachings of postmodernism, each person must create her own understanding of the universe, her own worldview. Humans are inherently good. Any flaws we might have are just a part of nature.

One of the darker nuances here is that many postmodernists suffer a loss of sense of self. If there is no overall meaning or lasting relationships in life, then everything is transient, changing, and fragmented. While we might suspect this to lead to lives of isolation, nothing could be further from the truth. Postmodernists prize their communities on the Web, in coffeehouses, and in literal communes. For these communities to survive, tolerance is essential.

Authority

Postmodernism recognizes no authority except for individual thought and experience. Any other authority would be based on a metanarrative created by people seeking power. All such metanarratives can and should be deconstructed. If a metanarrative such as Islam asserts that the Koran is divinely inspired, it must be false. The same goes for Christians claiming that the Bible is objectively true, authoritative for everyone.

This postmodern challenge to authority has influenced many Christians. Experiential worship is one of the demands of the day. No longer do people want to sit and be lectured or even entertained. They want to be involved in what's going on. Many churches have seen a renewed interest in liturgies for worship services that involve participants. There has also been a resurgence of what is called signs and wonders among some believers and churches. The spectrum of experiences runs from reciting the creeds of the early church to miracles and healings. So what happens when experiences conflict with the church's historical foundation for faith, the Bible?

Some Christians distinguish between the authority of God's Word and the supposed authority of the church. Some argue that each individual, not an organized church or denomination, has the right and responsibility to interpret the Bible for herself. (See individualism, page 173, and humanism, page 159.) If a group of individuals, interpreting the Bible through the grid of their experiences, choose to adopt some practices, a postmodern view of biblical interpretation would support them. Postmodernism takes to a new level a question debated in the Protestant Reformation five hundred years ago: Who interprets the Bible authoritatively? The hierarchy of the one true church? The academically trained leaders of a denomination? Communities of ordinary believers? Communities of believers in dialogue with those who have preceded them over the centuries? The individual, relying on reason? The individual, relying on experience? If we believe that the Holy Spirit guides true interpretation, how does the Holy Spirit speak?

For many postmodernists, the problem isn't the Bible, but communities or churches who interpret the Bible. Postmodernists deeply distrust institutions, because they are profoundly aware of how institutions can abuse authority. And it isn't hard to find examples of this in an institution like the Christian church, local or worldwide. In some churches, for example, members mask their feelings and act in ways that seem plastic, inauthentic, to postmodern eyes. Other churches play out competitions for power.

Yet even when churches are at their best, they still claim they have a God-given standard of what we're supposed to believe and how we're supposed to live. To an outlook like postmodernism that expects each individual to solve the world-view puzzle for himself, that stance is bound to seem rigid and controlling.

Salvation

Salvation in a postmodern context comes when people discover themselves. In other words, when a person finally understands who he or she is, there is a personal liberation experience. Through deconstruction, postmodernism aims to liberate people from all authority and give them a full understanding of self.

For Christians, any talk of salvation is directly tied to the authority in their lives—God, who speaks through the Bible. The metanarrative presented in the Bible states that finding your true self is impossible apart from Jesus Christ's birth, life, death, and resurrection. Sin, atonement, redemption, forgiveness—these are all part of the language of salvation as presented in the Bible. Without that authority in place, salvation can mean whatever the individual decides.

Time

Postmodernists view beliefs about heaven, hell, nirvana, or some other kind of afterlife as part of the metanarratives people create (positively) to give meaning to their lives or (negatively) to control what other people do. While postmodernism asserts that if an afterlife is real for you, that's fine, most postmodernists think this life is all there is. You should therefore experience all you can while you can.

Sometimes postmodernists become nihilists. **Nihilism*** is the belief that there is no meaning in anything. Philosophy is pointless. Science is pointless. Religion is pointless. Life is pointless. Philosopher Thomas Nagel argues that "life may be not only meaningless, but absurd."[3] Nihilism can be depressing, because it gives no hope for anything after this life and no real purpose for life itself.

Other postmodernists feel that the meaning they can create for themselves in this life is good enough, even terrific. Savor the experiences of this life, they say, and die with dignity. Death is just one more experience that the individual should define for himself. You have no obligation to live a minute longer than you want to.

Jesus

Jesus is a difficult figure for many postmodernists to figure out. He was a revolutionary teacher, a compassionate leader, and a man willing to die for his beliefs. His strength and inclusiveness are appealing. However, the context for Jesus Christ is found exclusively in the Bible, the metanarrative for Christians. And in the Bible, Jesus says some pretty outrageous things. C. S. Lewis commented,

> The idea of a great moral teacher saying what Christ said is out of the question. In my opinion, the only person who can say that sort of thing is either God or a complete lunatic suffering from that form of delusion which undermines the whole mind of man.[4]

To postmodernists, however, it's not necessary to take or leave the biblical portrait of Jesus as a whole. They feel free to take anything from Jesus' life and teachings that seems helpful and leave the rest. The Bible is a sourcebook of spiritual texts, not an authoritative whole, so postmodernists can accept a Jesus who loves and cares, while rejecting a Jesus who will judge all of humanity at the end of time. The Christian claim that Jesus is the only way to eternal life and the embodiment of absolute truth is simply part of a metanarrative designed to control people.

POSTMODERNISM AND CHRISTIANITY

Postmodernism's basic assumptions drive many of the ideas behind what we see on television, watch in movies, and read in books. Because it has become so influential, and because it challenges the claim that Jesus is the only way to eternal life and the embodiment of absolute truth, some Christians see it as a severe danger. On the other end of the spectrum, some have tried to baptize all things postmodern, making it their answer to frustrations with the current church climate. It's important, therefore, to understand the areas in which postmodernism and Christianity are poles apart, and the areas in which postmodernism gives Christians something to think about. If you were a missionary going to Russia, you'd have to learn and think Russian. In some ways, living as a Christian in America today may require learning to think postmodern.

Conversation is an important word in the postmodern vocabulary. Any attempt to *win* or *convert* someone to a particular way of thinking is seen as an intrusion. Christians have a particular way of thinking, but that doesn't necessarily have to lead to an overbearing way of interacting with people. In 1 Corinthians 9, the apostle Paul said he adapted to other people's cultures—Jewish or Gentile, weak or strong—in order to effectively spread the good news. Can Christians adopt a postmodern approach, without embracing postmodernism, in order to keep the conversation going?

Because postmodernists prefer to learn by doing, they pay more attention to how Christians live their faith than to how they talk about it. The Christian metanarrative makes post-modernists suspicious unless it comes from someone who lives with humility and confidence, victories and failures, laughter and tears, love and integrity. Even more appealing is experiencing groups of Christians like that.

In order to give you a better understanding of postmodernism, in the next few chapters we will examine a few more elements of this worldview that plays such a significant role in our culture today.

POSTMODERNISM GLOSSARY

Deconstruction—The postmodern idea of stripping away foundational concepts associated with ideas, religions, and philosophies. The goal in deconstruction is to get at the kernel of truth obscured by layers of human traditions. It assumes there is no such thing as objective truth.

Metanarrative—An overarching story that describes or explains life. For example, Christianity gives a holistic worldview shaped by the person of Christ. The story of evolution tells how chemicals evolved into lower and then higher life-forms through time, chance, and natural processes.

Nihilism—A belief that there is no purpose in anything. Rooted in naturalism, nihilism questions whether humans actually have any worth or purpose in life, because we are simply the products of natural processes.

Postmodernism—A philosophical concept whose adherents believe it has replaced modernity as the dominant worldview of our culture. Some argue that postmodernism is simply a logical outworking of modernistic thought.

Tolerance—In a postmodern context, an acceptance of any worldview, no matter how bizarre it might seem to some observers. Challenging someone's worldview or seeking to convert someone is seen as intolerant.

Truth Claims—Statements made by a religion or philosophy that are foundational for that worldview to work. Postmodernism looks at the vast variety of ideas and asserts that truth claims are inherently false. If they were true, postmodernism argues, there would not be as many truth claims in conflict.

Syncretism

I heard it before I saw it. The sound was the distinctive roar of the exhaust of a Harley-Davidson motorcycle. As my brother rounded the corner, I could see him grinning from ear to ear. He had been planning and saving for this bike for some time now, and the waiting was over. It wasn't as important as the birth of his children, but it ran a close second.

This was not our father's Harley-Davidson. This was a custom-built model that met my brother's exact specifications. He had accessed the Harley-Davidson website and customized his Fat Boy from the mirrors on the handlebars down to the studs on the saddlebags. He chose the color, type of suspension, exhaust pipes, and gas cap. No longer are you limited to just a few options; now you can put just about anything you want on a Harley if you're willing to pay. My brother was willing to pay, and the manufacturer was more than willing to take his money. The result is a beautiful motorcycle with details that appeal to my brother and my brother alone.

JUST WHAT YOU WANT

In the world of ideas, **syncretism*** allows for the same thing. The absence of a metanarrative gives a postmodernist permission to select as many philosophies as he likes to make an appealing worldview. In essence, syncretism meshes two or more perspectives into just what the particular person ordered.

Many believe syncretism to be the defining characteristic of American religion today. Americans seem to like the custom-order approach to religion. After some decades of secularism becoming an increasingly dominant influence in American culture, the 1960s saw the reemergence of spirituality. It was a spirituality that drew heavily on diverse and eclectic traditions, such as Eastern, Native American, and pre-Christian. There was never any attempt to create a coherent belief system; rather, this spirituality was interested in discovering and transforming the self. The assumption was that all religious roads head to the same place, that all religions ultimately have the same goals. (After reading this book, to what extent do you agree or disagree with this assumption?) Any contradictions were either overlooked or defined as a paradox.[1]

THE NEW/OLD AGE

These stirrings led directly into a discernible movement in the 1970s and '80s called "New Age." The **New Age***** movement combined Eastern philosophy and religion with Christianity and other spiritual ideas. This was the multilayered spirituality of the 1960s taken a step further.

New Age religion was a flash in the pan. You won't hear many people use the phrase "New Age" anymore, but you will often hear people refer to someone's "spirituality." In our day, it's almost expected that people embrace some form of spiritual experience. But the term *spirituality* makes it difficult sometimes to pin down actual beliefs. Juxtaposing Christian and pagan symbols, Mother Earth worship, and Satanism is not some far-fetched fiction; it's the age in which we live.

To make these pieces fit together, people routinely compartmentalize their lives. We are all probably guilty of this at one time or another. We live in a time when many people try to keep public life separate from private life and politics severed from personal convictions. Our lives are fragmented: We worship with one group of people, work with another, go to school with a third, and party with a fourth. So it's easy to practice Christianity at church on Sunday, adopt Buddhist stress management techniques to survive work, study biology and physics as a naturalist, and party on Saturday night as if none of it matters.

In custom-order spirituality, **pragmatism*** becomes the basis of the worldview. Pragmatism argues that as long as the result is good for you, then it shouldn't matter how you arrived at that result. A pragmatist would say, "If it works for you, go with it." (For more on pragmatism, see page 202.)

INEVITABLE, PROBLEMATIC, OR BOTH?

Some Christians in the postmodern discussion contend that syncretism is actually hard to avoid, if not impossible. Brian McLaren writes,

> Syncretism is usually what Christians who are thoroughly immersed in one culture talk about when Christianity is being influenced by other cultures. So, for example, modern Western Christians are very sensitive to a potential syncretism with postmodernity, but they are for the most part pretty oblivious to how enmeshed their version of the faith is with modernity.[2]

While this is by no means the majority position, it does represent those who believe it's essentially impossible to de-culture Christianity, because it always comes through a culture. First-century Judaism, they point out, wasn't only a religion, but also a culture. The same, they say, applies to Buddhism, Islam, and yes, even Christianity. They would be the first to say that some elements of any given culture are bad and some are good. However, says missiologist Lesslie Newbigin,

The question is whether these judgments arise from the gospel itself or from the cultural presuppositions of the person who makes the judgment. And, if one replies that they ought to be made only on the basis of the gospel itself, the reply must be that there is no such thing as a gospel which is not already culturally shaped.[3]

Sure, respond other Christians, but doesn't logic demand that we avoid mixing beliefs that inherently conflict? If Buddhism teaches that we'll be reincarnated after we die, but Christianity teaches that we'll face judgment and resurrection, can we believe both? And do we truly believe either one if we're living as though, for all practical purposes, this life is all there is?

Postmodernists question this concern with logical consistency. They're less interested in holding a worldview that is a coherent whole than in assembling a set of beliefs that works for them. In a world where electrons are both particles and waves, why should any paradox be a problem?

Keep all these thoughts in mind as we look at our worldview signposts.

WORLDVIEW SIGNPOSTS

God

Syncretism lets you customize God however you want. If you want a God of love, then find a religion or method to experience God as love. If you want a God that restricts himself from involvement in your personal life, find one. Want to avoid the staleness that must come from worshiping only one God? Choose as many as you like! Instead of the God revealed in the Bible or another religion's sacred book, you create God in your own image. Whatever you want, that's what you get.

The God created through syncretism is at the beck and call of your individual whims and fancies. That's good if you like to get your way and don't want a God who makes you uncomfortable. It's good if you don't mind inconsistency now and then. Your God will be psychologically satisfying. Whether or not you should bet your life on such a God is for you to decide.

Humanity and Authority

Syncretism elevates humanity to the highest point. No one can tell you what to do, because you are your own authority. You not only define your spirituality, you are the center of your own universe. Syncretism invites you to create a spiritual world or an existence that makes sense to you, for "you" are the king of your world.

Salvation

Christianity declares there is no salvation apart from Jesus Christ. Syncretism asserts that you and I must save ourselves. Since you create your spirituality, you set the terms for salvation. Do you have to work at it, or is it the universe's gift to you? You decide. Does it mean becoming a better person or just feeling okay about yourself? That's up to you.

Many people take this idea and live a very moral life. Others apply an ethic that chooses the path of least resistance when faced with a moral dilemma. In the end, the hope is that good outweighs bad, and they will gain entrance into whatever eternity they have invented for themselves.

Time

Emphasizing the here and now, syncretism stresses the importance of living in the moment. If you choose portions of religions that have more of a historical cast, perhaps you'll reflect on the past and the future. But for most people, syncretism helps them live day by day. Like many postmodernists, they seek experience after experience, hoping to discover the missing pieces of their spiritualism. Each new adrenaline high or educational discovery could be the next vista where true meaning can be found.

Using religion to cope with life's realities produces all manner of interpretations of the end of time. They range from nihilism to a literal heaven and hell. Because syncretists create their own meaning in life, most of these visions of the afterlife are positive, especially when applied to themselves. Some syncretists like the idea of the world's Hitlers facing eternal suffering, but few think anybody they like deserves such a fate. Some believe in reincarnation, but few expect that they or their friends will come back next time as a toad because they've been self-centered this time around.

The Christian worldview too emphasizes living in the present moment. However, this emphasis is informed by an expectation of heaven. That hope is a guide in being fully present in this moment, not worrying about tomorrow, and letting the past be the past as you press on.

Jesus

Jesus is the best part of syncretism. He has been co-opted by so many religious and spiritual constructions that there's a Jesus out there somewhere for everybody. It's always an interesting exercise to look at how Jesus is portrayed in art. For some,

Jesus is the blue-eyed blond of nineteenth-century American Protestantism. Others see him as the Jesus of the Sacred Heart. Some like him gentle and meek, holding a lamb and smiling at a child. Others like a more muscular, manly Jesus. He can be a political activist or serene and meditative. You pick.

What are we to do here? Just who is the real Jesus? Lesslie Newbigin argues,

> "Jesus" is not a name to which we can attach any character we like to imagine. Jesus is the name of a man of whom we have information in the books of the New Testament interpreted (as they must be) in the light of books which were Jesus' own scriptures. The Jesus of whom the New Testament writers bear witness is not an inaccessible figure.[4]

SYNCRETISM AND CHRISTIANITY

Today there is an openness in our world to spiritual things that did not exist seventy-five years ago. For some Christians, this is lamentable; for others, it is refreshing. One thing is for certain: Attempts to engage people in a postmodern, syncretistic context require words like patience, humility, longsuffering, and love (see Galatians 5). As we mentioned in the section on postmodernism, of supreme importance these days is the authenticity of your personal life. Another way of saying this is, "Do you practice what you preach?" Think of the image of a fellow traveler. If you're willing to take this stance alongside others as they struggle in their search for meaning, you just might be invited along for the ride.

And when you encounter ideas and customs from other worldviews that appeal to you, you'll have to decide what to do with them. Some Christians believe any degree of syncretism is wrong. They don't allow Christmas trees in their homes because decorating a tree in the home was originally part of a winter ritual practiced by pre-Christian Europeans for whom some trees were sacred. They don't decorate eggs or eat chocolate bunnies for Easter because eggs and bunnies were pre-Christian fertility symbols.

Other Christians believe we can assess each non-Christian idea and custom to decide whether it fits or conflicts with Christian faith. Can a Christian practice yoga for her health without embracing the Hindu spiritual beliefs behind the breathing and body poses? Some say yes, others no.

You'll also need to decide how important logical consistency is to you. For instance, it's inconsistent to take your sexual ethics from naturalism while believing in the miracle of Jesus' resurrection and calling him the Son of God. But if inconsistency doesn't bother you, you may opt to do the one while believing the other.

Finally, you'll need to decide what authority grounds your life. Do you build your life on your desires as an individual? On the teachings of Buddha? On science? On God speaking through the Bible? If you feel free to select what you like from all of these, just be aware that by default you've chosen yourself as your authority.

SYNCRETISM GLOSSARY

New Age—A religious system in the twentieth century that combined elements of Christianity with Eastern spirituality.

Pragmatism—A philosophical system that puts the emphasis on the end result rather than on the issues that lead to the result.

Syncretism—An attempt to blend elements of varying philosophies or religions to make a new system that works for the individual.

Pragmatism

Almost every story line has some dependable characters and moments. As characters go, look for the hero, the person in distress (this could be male or female), the villain(s), and the people around them, the community. As for moments, look for a leaving of home or familiar settings, followed by a series of tests, and finally a moment of crisis where the hero or heroine has to decide what he or she is willing to do and not willing to do. Many stories, if they follow a traditional line, have the hero or heroine adopting a "whatever it takes" mentality in this moment of crisis. The conclusion of the story reveals what this resolve looks like; the hero gets the girl, the heroine gets the guy, or the knights discover the Holy Grail. Everyone returns to some semblance of home and presumably lives happily ever after.

Pragmatism is a bit like the "whatever it takes" mentality. In life we experience challenges and obstacles that make it hard to achieve our goals. Pragmatism asserts that the goal or the result is what is most important, not how you attain it. Of all the philosophies, pragmatism just may be the most distinctly American. It seems to have its roots in the ideas of Charles Pierce and William James in the 1870s. Another name readily thought of when pragmatism is mentioned is that of John Dewey, who played a key role in the development of educational philosophy.

Although there are several varieties of this philosophy, the common denominator among them is how truth is viewed. Pragmatism emphasizes that there is no absolute truth. On the contrary, the truth or meaning of something can be detected from its practical results or consequences.

SITUATIONAL AND COMMUNITY ETHICS

The American philosopher Richard Rorty expressed many of the modern ideas about pragmatism. He too believed there is no such thing as objective truth. Instead, he argued that truth changes depending on the context. In other words, each of us has to cope with situations that come our way. Because the context of the situation is different for each person, we apply different standards to solve the problems we face. Rorty believed that "truth" is simply a concept or an idea we use to justify our actions in light of the situations in which we find ourselves.

Rorty's emphasis was practicality. If we're picky about principles, the quest for the truth to solve a particular problem could take months, if not years. Rorty saw this as unnecessary, so he devised a shortcut: Just get to the goal no matter what. Any action you take can be justified by simply asserting that your truth dictated your actions and the end result is really all that matters.

Let that sentence sink in just a little. The end result is all that matters. Any action can be justified.

Distilled to this level, pragmatism loses a little of its glow. It creates a world of individuals seeking nothing other than meeting their basic cravings and desires, while justifying themselves along the way. Rorty would readily challenge this interpretation, because he believed that the context that determines the way we understand truth is given by our community. In other words, if you are an American citizen, you have to pay taxes. You might find unique ways to pay your taxes, such as robbing a bank, but because robbing a bank is wrong in our society/community, this would not be an appropriate way to pay your taxes. If we lived in a society/community that did not consider it against the law to rob banks, then we could be completely justified in paying our taxes by that route. According to Rorty, truth is always determined by our community of interpretation—not just by each of us as an individual.

TELLING YOUR STORY OR TELLING A STORY

Rorty's pragmatism invites creative problem solving. Let's say you decide to write a portion of your memoirs for a class presentation. The pragmatic approach makes the single most important thing to be the final grade, not what you might *learn* from doing the research. You live in a culture that places a premium not only on academic achievement, but also on a good story. The end result, a good grade or riveting story, is all that matters. *How* you get it does not.

You sit down at the keyboard and begin reflecting on certain experiences in your life. After some time, you begin to realize that up to this point, your life has been rather uneventful, actually quite plain. How is this going to help you get the grade you desire? You really need to do well on this assignment. Your GPA is slipping and you're in danger of losing your scholarship. A crisis moment for the hero or heroine looks you squarely in the face.

You decide to do "whatever it takes." You begin to take extreme liberty with the facts of your life, even falsifying some accounts in an effort to make your past dark and gritty, filled with impossible odds. When you present your memoirs to the class, you get rave reviews and the professor extends you an A.

You got the desired result, and presumably everyone should live happily ever after. Right? Yes, from the standpoint of pragmatism. No, from a standpoint that views certain principles as objectively right. From this standpoint of objective principles, altering the facts of your life is not memoir; it's fiction. Presenting a fictional account as factual is lying and cheating.

It's wrong. But in pragmatism, issues of right and wrong ebb and flow with the situation.

For Rorty, a pragmatist avoids total relativism because he makes his decisions within the context of a community that interprets what is true and false, right and wrong. But what if we find ourselves with one foot in one community (say, a Christian one) and another foot in a community with quite different views (say, students at a naturalist or secular humanist college campus)? If we're pragmatists, then there is no overarching truth (metanarrative) and no authority that tells us which community to listen to when we're doing a class assignment. We're at a loss when it comes to competing truth claims from two different communities of interpretation. In practice, we might choose the community whose rules make it easiest for us to reach our goal.

WORLDVIEW SIGNPOSTS

God

Pragmatism shares postmodernism's perspective on God. God may exist or he/she/it may not. If a concept of God is working for you, great! If it's not, great! If God is working out for you, then it's also possibly a God as defined by your community. If you attend an evangelical church, you will have one perspective of who God is. If you are a Hindu, you have another idea of God. According to postmodernism, both perspectives are right, even if they conflict.

Humanity and Authority

In this portion of the postmodern worldview, individuals within a community function as the ultimate authority. In taking this position, we become the ones who create truth and meaning. Even with pragmatism's emphasis on the need for a community of interpretation, you can see some of the issues that could pose a problem. How many social "cliques" have you encountered? What about a group of people in a community or neighborhood who interpret truth in a way that harms other people? It pays to consider the lines from the *Sesame Street* song: "Oh, who are the people in your neighborhood?"

Salvation

Rorty and other pragmatists lean toward utopian ideals. They believe that if institutions — churches, schools, governments, businesses — would stop advancing their perspectives about truth and authority, the world would balance itself and develop an "appropriate mixture."[1] Different communities would police themselves as far as what was right and wrong. Diverse groups would tolerate those who don't share their values and beliefs. In this utopian vision, humans would finally escape the bounds of objective truth. Salvation would be discovered through human freedom.

Time

For the pragmatist, time is simply a unit of measurement. It marks the rising and setting of the sun, nothing more. We exist within a framework bound by time, but this has little to do with the realities of attaining our goals and dreams. We must accomplish all we can today, because there are never any guarantees for tomorrow. By investing our time wisely within our community, we transform the world, moving it ever closer to the realization of the true aim of humanity in a postmodern system: freedom.

Jesus

Very much like the pragmatist view of God, Jesus is defined by our community of interpretation. For many communities, this means appropriating the love and grace of Jesus, not his other divine attributes like his holiness and wrath. You keep the parts of Jesus that work for you and jettison the parts that don't. In ways similar to syncretism, you customize Jesus to be what you want him to be — maybe a means to an end, a way to feel better about yourself, or just someone to consult occasionally on really difficult matters.

PRAGMATISM AND CHRISTIANITY

Pragmatism asserts that truth is completely open to interpretation. There are no firm ethical principles with which we can all start as we approach the wide variety of situations life throws at us. By contrast, the Christian tradition says that there are principles that applied in ancient Israel and still apply in modern America. Applying the principles to new situations can require wisdom and creative thinking, but the principles themselves come from an objective source: God, through the Bible.

In the Christian tradition, lying is wrong, even to get a good grade and protect your scholarship. Does that mean there is never, ever a situation when lying might be okay? Say you were hiding Jews during World War II, and Nazis came to your door and asked, straight out, are you hiding Jews here? Some Christians would say you have to tell the truth even then. Others would say that there's another ethical principle in play: love your neighbor. When two ethical principles collide in a situation ("don't lie" and "love your neighbor"), the one the Bible treats as primary trumps the other. So in this rare situation, you lie to save some people's lives. But rare situations like this one don't invalidate the principle about lying.

That's how Christian ethical reasoning works. Notice that it's reasoning (meaning brain work and heart work) based on objective principles, and that the goal (saving lives) isn't selfish. You're not lying to save your skin. You're lying to save someone else's skin.

Pragmatism looks for shortcuts. Christianity views shortcuts with suspicion, especially when the goal is self-interest. The Bible is full of stories in which pragmatism gets people into trouble (check out Genesis 16, for instance). As Paul says in 1 Corinthians 6:12, "Just because something is technically legal doesn't mean that it's spiritually appropriate" (The Message).

But ultimately, if your life is about short-term self-interest, pragmatism is going to look appealing. So maybe it's helpful to think not just about means, but also about ends. What's your goal? The Bible lays out love as both means and end. The highest goal of life, from this point of view, is to love God and love your neighbor — that is, to seek what is truly good for God and truly good for your neighbor, even if it sometimes costs you. Pragmatism argues that there's no way to know what's good for God, and it's debatable what's really good for your neighbor, so you're better off aiming at something easier, like what you want. The Bible claims to tell you what's good for God (worship, obedience) and for your neighbor (truth, generosity, justice, forgiveness), while admitting that going after what you want might feel better a lot of the time.

You pick: What's your goal? Is it all about you?

The End, and Maybe the Beginning

> We shall not cease from exploration
> And the end of all our exploring
> Will be to arrive where we started
> And know the place for the first time.

—T. S. Eliot, *Four Quartets*: "Little Gidding"

Remember, the word *worldview* literally means the way the world is viewed. Unless you're on another planet looking down on the rest of us, then you are a part of that view. The way you live—your choices, decisions, and direction—is bound up in your worldview. *To discover your worldview is to discover who you are.* That sentence is taken from the introduction to this book. So in some way, we're ending up where we started. Any desire to really find yourself, discover who you are, become who you were created to be—you describe it with your phrase of choice—regardless, it begins with thinking about how you view the world.

The goal throughout this book has been to present the facts, minus the spin, and respect your ability to think and reason for yourself. The hope has been that you would not "cease from exploration" once you've finished this book, but continue on this journey of discovery. The sections presented here can continue to be reference points for you as you wrestle with worldviews and their implications.

We live in a time when we believe we think for ourselves. The evidence, however, seems to be that we do not. We blindly accept the thoughts and thought processes that are handed to us by parents, teachers, the church, the cinema, our friends, and the list goes on. These worldviews affect everything from our finances to how we raise our children and what legacy, if any, we seek to leave for future generations. If you truly desire to think for yourself, then go for it. Start thinking.

We also live in a time when people are more aware than ever of different worldviews. This awareness, however, does not equal understanding. This awareness is something your grandparents knew nothing of, but it is the world in which you live and into which your children will one day be born. Start thinking.

The "worldview signposts" we've used — such as humanity, authority, time, and salvation — are wonderful prompters for your thoughts. We, the authors, also challenge you to consider God and Jesus Christ in those thoughts. We are unapologetically Christian. We have struggled with our own worldviews, as well as those handed to us by others, and have arrived at the place where *we* believe we started: God. Please don't hear a "got it all together" mentality; we continue to wrestle with and strive to be aware of worldviews every day. Some days we see them, and some days we miss them. While there are definite contrasts between worldviews, there is also occasional great subtlety, and we believe it requires a lifelong commitment to *thinking* to live fully in this world. We are your fellow pilgrims.

LIVE THE QUESTIONS

The late autumn of 1902 found one Franz Xaver Kappus writing to the German poet Rainer Maria Rilke. Kappus was on the brink of entering a profession, yet found himself questioning not only his inclinations, but his identity as well. Over the next five years, Kappus and Rilke corresponded regularly. At one point, Kappus appeared frustrated at all the thinking to be done, and Rilke responded:

> Be patient toward all that is unresolved in your heart and try to love the questions themselves like locked rooms and like books that are written in a very foreign tongue. Do not now seek the answers, which cannot be given you because you would not be able to live them. And the point is, to live everything. Live the questions now. Perhaps you will gradually . . . live along some distant day into the answer."[1]

Live out the questions associated with worldviews. Test them, try them, and prove them if you can. Do not yield just because something seems unresolved. Continue to live the questions. An airtight worldview often indicates a lack of truly critical thinking or a childish naiveté; both are dangerous in their own right. Let the word *gradual* guide you as you discover what you believe deeply enough to bet your life on. Pay attention to ways your actions reveal what you really believe, especially when those actions and deep notions don't square with other beliefs that are important to you.

Our prayer is that this commitment to thinking and discovery leads you someday into the answer. Godspeed. Keep thinking.

Worldview Legend

Use the chart that follows to gain a quick reference to the worldviews presented in this book. It is organized according to the six worldview components we explored.

	God	Humanity	Salvation	Authority	Time	Jesus
Christianity	God is a tri-unity of Father, Son, and Holy Spirit. The divine Creator of everything, he is omnipotent, omniscient, and in control of every aspect of the world around us. Ever present, God desires a personal relationship with all humans.	Humans are fallen creatures who suffer under the curse of sin. We are created for fellowship with God, but our sin completely separates us from God.	Salvation is only found in the person of Jesus Christ, who died on the cross, was buried, and rose on the third day. God planned for the incarnation of Christ to redeem humanity even before he created the world. The offer of salvation is free to anyone who accepts the message of the gospel.	All people are subject to the authority of God whether they realize it or not. The Bible is God's revelation of himself to humanity. In it, we discover how we are supposed to live.	God is outside the boundaries of time, but he created time for us. He knows the set moment when time will cease to exist. A literal heaven awaits God's children just as a literal hell is prepared for those who disobey him.	Jesus is the incarnate Son of God, who is both 100 percent human and 100 percent divine. Jesus provided salvation for everyone through his death and resurrection. He reigns with God from heaven.

	God	Humanity	Salvation	Authority	Time	Jesus
Hinduism	There are many gods, but all of them are manifestations of the Absolute, the main force of the cosmos. Most Hindus practice *henotheism*, which elevates one of the many gods above the others without denying the existence of the other deities.	Humans contain a part of the Absolute in their being. The cycle of reincarnation rids a person of bad *karma* so he or she can return to the Absolute. Each individual chooses the path he or she thinks will lead to that return.	There are three main paths to *moksha* and liberation from the cycles of reincarnation: the path of works, the path of knowledge, and the path of devotion. Each of these paths contains some truths that help to dissolve the debt of karma so moksha can be achieved.	There are two classes of scriptures: *Shruti*, that which is heard, and *Smriti*, that which is remembered. Shruti texts such as the four Vedas are understood to have the highest level of inspiration. Smriti texts, while considered inspired, do not carry the same weight as the Vedas and give examples of how to live the appropriate life.	Hindus, along with people of other Eastern religions, have a cyclical view of time. Things keep repeating. Even at death, life is reborn unless a Hindu attains moksha, at which point *nirvana* begins. Nirvana is simply returning to the Absolute and ceasing to exist as an individual. Like a drop of water in the ocean, when a Hindu finds nirvana, there are no longer any distinguishing features of personhood.	Jesus is viewed as an avatar of *Vishnu* or *Shiva* in some variations of Hinduism. Others believe he teaches an alternate way to reach the Absolute. By following the teachings of Jesus, a person can hope to be reincarnated as a Hindu and be one step closer to moksha.

	God	Humanity	Salvation	Authority	Time	Jesus
Buddhism	The Absolute, an impersonal force in the universe, is recognized as the only reality. Buddhists recognize the existence of lesser deities that are both male and female. Some branches of Buddhism believe that *Buddha* was divine.	Buddhists place value on all life. Humans and other life-forms are equal in the amount of *karma* they possess. Humans can experience enlightenment by following the path that Buddha revealed to his followers.	Through meditation and right living, a person can accumulate enough positive karma to escape the cycle of *samsara*. This takes quite a bit of personal effort to accomplish over many lifetimes.	The teaching of Buddha is recorded and commented upon in the *suttas* forms the basic authority structure for Buddhism. It is still very broad, because some branches empha-size the authority of personal expe-rience.	There is no such thing as heaven or an end to time. Everyone is trapped in the cycle of *samsara*, or reincarna-tion, until the accumulation of enough positive karma gives one the ability to be enlightened and experience *nirvana*. Nirvana is a state of being, not a place.	Buddhism says little about Jesus, because Buddha lived before Jesus. Most Buddhists regard Jesus as a historical figure who may have been a Buddha or a *bodhisatva*. His teachings contain wisdom.

	God	Humanity	Salvation	Authority	Time	Jesus
Islam	*Allah* is stressed to be the one god. He rules earth from a distance and does not stoop to engage humans on a personal level. *Muhammad* is the final prophet and mouthpiece of Allah.	The role of humanity is to submit to Allah and to serve as his ambassadors on earth.	Salvation occurs by recitation of the *shahadah* and living a life of submission to Allah.	The *Koran* is the highest authority for life and practice in *Islam*. Other texts are recognized, but the Koran in its original Arabic is the infallible and inerrant words of Allah.	Time is under the control of Allah, who is viewed as the creator. At the end of time, *Muslims* believe they will go to heaven, a literal place with varying levels. The more you follow Allah's teachings on earth, the closer you will be to him in heaven.	Jesus was a prophet who pointed the way to Muhammad.
Naturalism	*Naturalism* usually denies that God exists. Truth resides in human progress and science.	Naturalism affirms that humans are the product solely of time and chance. Human beings are no different from any other animal on the planet.	Naturalists believe that humans can produce their own salvation from their earthly problems by promoting education and scientific development. Any vestiges of religion are to be eradicated.	Humans form the basis for the authority structure of naturalism. There is no need to look outside ourselves, because we are the final authority.	The only thing that is eternal in the universe is matter. There is no afterlife; once you die, you cease to exist.	Jesus existed, but only as a historical figure. Miracles and supernatural occurrences are scientifically impossible, so the biblical records of them are legends.

	God	Humanity	Salvation	Authority	Time	Jesus
Darwinism	Charles Darwin's theory of evolution attempts to describe the process of creation without a Creator God.	Darwinian thinkers believe that humans are essentially animals. They deny that we are either good or bad. As the product of thousands of years of evolution, we simply live and then die.	There is no salvation in a Darwinist system. We can contribute to society as much as we can during our lives, but natural processes largely govern what happens in the world.	Science is the ultimate authority for Darwinists. The only things trustworthy are those proven through science or physics.	Because there have been many evolutionary modifications, it took billions of years to get to where we are today. Your existence is simply a blip on the radar of time.	Darwinists think Jesus was simply a good man who lived in our historical past. Jesus' divine claims in the Bible are legends.
The Sexual Revolution	There is great variance here. Many who embraced the sexual revolution claim a definite belief in God. Others see this as a glaring contradiction.	We are basically animals. Humans should simply do what comes naturally to them. Sex takes on the role as one of the most significant human experiences one can have.	Salvation is the direct result of attaining freedom. Freedom of expression is ultimately attained by removing the traditional taboos and moral relics of the past.	The sexual revolution claims you are your own authority. You set the rules for sexual behavior and contact.	The sexual revolution thinks of humans as here today, gone tomorrow. We should eat, drink, and be merry because we may die.	The early part of the sexual revolution saw Jesus as leading a revolution against authority and stuffy religion. The more Christians pointed to the picture of Jesus in the Bible, those embracing the sexual revolution moved away from the person of Jesus.

	God	Humanity	Salvation	Authority	Time	Jesus
Secularism	Takes either an *agnostic* or *atheistic* position when referring to the concept of God. Ultimately, humans are viewed as the masters of their own destiny.	Humans determine the values of life and in essence are the gods of secularism. Science is the tool used to reinforce the superiority of humans above other elements of nature.	Salvation is found through evolution and human effort. Eradicating theism and irrational ideas will aid the evolutionary shift as humans attain a final evolutionary utopia.	Humans are their own authority in secularism. *Utilitarianism* is the basic ethic: What is the greatest good for the greatest number of people?	Humans appear in time because they are part of the ebb and flow of nature. There is no ultimate purpose for life except to enjoy it. At death, a person simply ceases to exist.	Jesus was simply a teacher or a good person. The teachings of the church are gross misrepresentations of the true teachings of Christ.
Humanism	According to secular humanists, it is simply irrational to believe that such a deity could even exist.	Humanists believe people are the solution to all of the issues in the world. The individual is elevated to near-divine status. The concept of the divine human is moderated only somewhat by an insistence that we should be selfless toward others.	Salvation happens when humans work together for the good of every person on the planet. Humanists believe that eventually people will police themselves.	The basic authority of humanism is the individual. There is no external system of laws imposed by a divine Being.	This is the only time you have. Many advocate living in the moment: Do anything and everything that makes you happy as long as you don't hurt others.	Jesus was a good example for all of humanity, but in the end, he was just a good man. The Jesus presented in the New Testament is a myth and never existed.

	God	Humanity	Salvation	Authority	Time	Jesus
Individualism	God may exist, but for practical purposes, we can live without the aid of God. God either cannot or will not participate directly in the life of any single person.	Your power and your will get you where you want to go. Human life struggles against extreme odds to make a place for itself in this world. Those who fight, succeed.	Individualists discover salvation through achievement and fame. For many who accept individualism as a worldview, only fame or notoriety is eternal.	Individualism stresses the *autonomy* of each person and makes the assertion that we are our own authority. Freedom is the highest value.	At the end of life, we cease to exist. This leads some to feel hopeless when life is isolated against the backdrop of time. Life appears worthless to many who embrace individualism, especially if they lead ordinary lives.	Individualism struggles with accepting Jesus as Lord because that means surrendering personal rights in obedience to another.
Postmodernism	*Postmodernism* approaches the concept of God from the perspective of the individual. It is not uncommon for postmodernism to assert that some form of a divine Being does exist. The ideas of God held by postmodernists are often *syncretistic*.	Postmodernism has a high view of humanity. In postmodernism, each person must create his or her own understanding of the universe. There are no ideas of sin. Instead, humans are inherently good and only seeking to find their place in the universe.	Salvation in a postmodern context comes when an individual fully realizes himself or herself. When a person finally understands who he or she is, then there is a personal liberation experience. Through *deconstruction*, postmodernism aims for liberation from all authority and a full understanding of self.	In postmodern thought, there is no authority except for individual humans and human experience. Postmodernists mistrust belief systems that claim to have truths that are true for everyone, because such systems tend to be used to gain power over other people.	For most postmodernists, once you die, there is no afterlife. This is it. For others who borrow from religious traditions, the afterlife is essentially positive.	Jesus is a difficult figure for postmodernism to figure out. He was a great teacher, a leader, and a person even willing to die for what he believed in, but some of his teachings are too difficult. Jesus also made exclusive claims to holding truth. That does not fit the postmodern paradigm.

	God	Humanity	Salvation	Authority	Time	Jesus
Syncretism	*Syncretism* provides you the opportunity to choose the God you want. Whatever elements you think are positive for a God to have, you can attribute those to your God.	Syncretism elevates humanity to the highest point. No one can tell you what to do, because you are your own authority. You not only define your own spirituality, you are the center of your own universe.	Syncretism asserts that you and I must save ourselves. Since you create your spirituality, you set the terms for salvation.	Syncretism invites you to create a spiritual world or an existence that makes sense to you. You are king of that world. You dictate what happens in it.	Seeking experiences that define the missing pieces of their spiritualism, syncretists stress the importance of living in the moment.	Since syncretism invites people to create their own image of God, the same goes for their understanding of Jesus. You can take the parts of Jesus you like and leave the rest.
Pragmatism	Because *pragmatism* doesn't accept objective truth, it makes no difference how you define God. Your community may define him as real or not.	Pragmatism elevates humanity to near-godlike status, because every person determines reality and truth for himself or herself.	If institutions would stop advancing their perspectives about truth, the world would balance itself. When conflicting claims or values are discovered among communities, tolerance is the name of the game.	Individuals within a community function as the ultimate authority. We become the ones who create truth and meaning.	Time is simply a unit of measurement. It marks the rising and setting of the sun, nothing more. We exist within a framework bound by time, but this has little to do with the realities of attaining our goals and dreams.	Jesus is defined by the community. For some, this means appropriating the love and grace of Jesus, not his other divine attributes such as holiness and wrath. Expect to find people who have customized Jesus to fit the image they want.

Notes

A Collapsible House

1. See Matthew 7:24-27.

2. Ecclesiastes 1:9, NIV.

What Is a Worldview?

1. Just in case you have an inner nerd like I do, the German word is *weltanschauung.*

2. For more on Antony Flew's move to theism, see Habermas and Flew, "My Pilgrimage from Atheism to Theism," *Philosophia Christi*, vol. 6, no. 2 (winter 2005): 197–212.

3. See 2 Corinthians 5:17.

4. G. K. Chesterton, *Heretics* (New York: John Lane, 1919), 6.

5. Chesterton, 6.

God

1. See 1 John 4:8.

2. Psalm 139:7-8,13-14.

Salvation

1. John 14:6.

Authority

1. 2 Timothy 3:16-17, emphasis added.

2. Hebrews 4:12.

3. See Matthew 22:37-40.

Time

1. Dorothy L. Sayers, *The Divine Comedy Cantica II: Purgatory* (New York: Penguin, 1955), 16.

Notes

Jesus

1. John 14:9.
2. See Philippians 2:10-11.
3. See Hebrews 4:15.

Introduction to Theism

1. David Alexander, *Star Trek Creator* (New York: Roc, 1995), 422.
2. Henry David Thoreau, *The Maine Woods*, ed. Joseph J. Moldenhauer (Princeton, NJ: Princeton University Press, 1972), 121.
3. Acts 17:28, NIV.

Hinduism

1. See Herbert Ellinger, *Hinduism* (London: SCM Press, 1996), 3; Peter Occhiogrosso, *The Joy of Sects* (New York: Doubleday, 1994), 2.
2. Mohandas Gandhi as cited in David S. Noss and John B. Noss, *A History of the World's Religions*, 9th ed. (Upper Saddle River, NJ: Prentice Hall, 1994), 148.
3. Ellinger, 9.

Buddhism

1. Dates in China and Japan place Buddha's birth date around 1067 BC. Other traditions place the date around 623–624. 563 BC seems to be the accepted date in the West. See Peter Occhiogrosso, *The Joy of Sects* (New York: Doubleday, 1994), 87.
2. Malcolm David Eckel, *Buddhism* (Oxford: Oxford University Press, 2002), 6–7.
3. "The Word of the Buddha," from *A Buddhist Bible*, ed. Dwight Goddard (Boston: Beacon Press, 1994), 59.
4. See comments by Walter Martin, *Kingdom of the Cults* (Minneapolis: Bethany, 1987), 311.
5. See Todd T. Lewis, "Tantra," *Buddhism: The Illustrated Guide*, ed. Kevin Trainor (New York: Oxford University Press, 2001), 162–173.

6. Eckel, 45.

7. Thich Nhat Hanh, *Going Home: Jesus and Buddha as Brothers* (New York: Riverhead Books, 1999), 195. See also the discussion in Richard Hughes Seager, *Buddhism in America* (New York: Columbia University Press, 1999), 221–225.

8. Hanh, 91.

Islam

1. This statistic quoted by Gayle Young, "Fast-growing Islam winning converts in Western world," *CNN.com*, April 14, 1997, www.cnn.com/WORLD/9704/14/egypt.islam.

2. Ed. Arthur Jeffery, *Islam: Muhammad and His Religion* (New York: Liberal Arts Press, 1958), 19.

3. George Braswell Jr., *Islam: Its Prophet, Peoples, Politics and Power* (Nashville: Broadman, Holman, 1996), 31.

4. Seyyed Hossein Nasr, *Islam: Religion, History, and Civilization* (San Francisco: HarperSanFrancisco, 2003), 92.

5. Nasr, 97.

6. Sura 6:102.

7. Braswell, 44.

8. Sura 57:3.

9. Nasr, 60. Nasr points out that "the Divine reveals itself as the Immanent only by virtue of having been first known and experienced as the Transcendent."

10. Malcolm X, *The Autobiography of Malcolm X*, as quoted in Peter Occhiogrosso, *The Joy of Sects* (New York: Doubleday, 1994), 438.

Naturalism and Materialism

1. See Paul Moser and J. D. Trout, *Contemporary Materialism* (New York: Routledge, 1995), 13–14.

2. Wendell Berry, *The Unsettling of America: Culture and Agriculture* (San Francisco: Sierra Club Books, 1986), 11.

Notes

3. Barbara MacKinnon, "Experimentalism and Naturalism of J. Dewey," *American Philosophy: A Historical Anthology* (Albany, NY: State University of New York Press, 1985), 261.

Darwinsim

1. Max Tegmark and Marcus Chown, "Anything Goes," *New Scientist*, vol. 158, no. 2137 (June 6, 1998): 26–30.

2. David Quammen, "Was Darwin Wrong?" *National Geographic*, November 2004, http://magma.nationalgeographic.com/ngm/0411/feature1/fulltext.html.

3. The various evangelical Christian understandings of the Bible's inerrancy are discussed in *Theology: Think for Yourself About What You Believe* in the TH1NK REFERENCE COLLECTION.

The Sexual Revolution

1. C. S. Lewis, *Mere Christianity* (New York: Macmillan, 1952), 89–90.

Secularism

1. *The Random House College Dictionary*, rev. ed., s.v. "Secular."

2. Kellie Sisson Snider, "ACLU History," 2002, http://arar.essortment.com/acluamericanci_rmal.htm.

3. William Hamilton, "The Death of God Theologies Today," in Thomas J. J. Altizer and William Hamilton, *Radical Theology and the Death of God* (Indianapolis: Bobbs-Merrill, 1966), 27.

4. Carl Sagan as quoted by David A. Noebel, *Understanding the Times* (Eugene, OR: Harvest House, 1994), 52.

5. Lesslie Newbigin, *The Gospel in a Pluralist Society* (Grand Rapids, MI: Eerdmans, 1989), 220.

Humanism

1. The first draft of this document was framed in 1933. In 1973, the *Humanist Manifesto II* was recorded. Signers of the 1973 version include noted scientist Carl Sagan and author Isaac Asimov.

2. This is a paraphrase of what is found at American Humanist Association, *Humanism and Its Aspirations*, 2003, www.americanhumanist.org/3/humanditsaspirations.php.

3. American Humanist Association.

4. The Center for Religious Humanism, "Vision," www.imagejournal.org/crh/vision.asp.

5. Eds. E. D. Hirsch Jr., Joseph F. Kett, and James Trefil, *The New Dictionary of Cultural Literacy*, 3rd ed. (New York: Houghton Mifflin, 2002), www.bartleby.com/59/5/manisthemeas.html.

Individualism

1. Ed. Richard Poirier, *Ralph Waldo Emerson: A Critical Edition of the Major Works* (New York: Oxford University Press, 1990), 133.

2. John 12:24-26.

3. See 1 Corinthians 6:19-20.

4. See 1 Corinthians 12:12-27.

5. Jean Vanier, *Community and Growth* (New York: Paulist Press, 1989), 18–19.

Postmodernism

1. J. Richard Middleton and Brian J. Walsh, *Truth Is Stranger Than It Used to Be* (Downers Grove, IL: InterVarsity, 1995), 71.

2. Some 88 percent of all Americans view themselves as religious, although it is sometimes uncertain what is meant by the term "religious." See *Newsweek*, September 5, 2005, for an interesting discussion of spirituality in America.

3. Thomas Nagel, *What Does It All Mean? A Very Short Introduction to Philosophy* (New York: Oxford University Press, 1987), 101.

4. C. S. Lewis, *God in the Dock: Essays on Theology and Ethics*, ed. Walter Hooper (Grand Rapids, MI: Eerdmans, 1970), 158.

Syncretism

1. Eddie Gibbs, *ChurchNext: Quantum Changes in How We Do Ministry* (Downers Grove, IL: InterVarsity, 2000), 125.

2. Brain D. McLaren, *A New Kind of Christian: A Tale of Two Friends on a Spiritual Journey* (San Francisco: Jossey-Bass, 2001), 78.

3. Lesslie Newbigin, *The Gospel in a Pluralist Society* (Grand Rapids, MI: Eerdmans, 1989), 186.

4. Newbigin, 192.

Pragmatism

1. Stanley Grenz, *A Primer on Postmodernism* (Grand Rapids: Eerdmans, 1996), 160.

The End, and Maybe the Beginning

1. Rainer Maria Rilke, *Letters to a Young Poet*, trans. M. D. Norton (New York: Norton, 1954), 35.

About the Authors

JOHN M. YEATS teaches Church History at Southwestern Baptist Theological Seminary. He earned his degrees from Trinity Evangelical Divinity School, The Southern Baptist Theological Seminary, Oxford University, and The Criswell College. He has served congregations in Texas, Indiana, and Illinois.

Currently, John lives in Fort Worth, Texas, with his wife, three kids, and two dogs.

JOHN BLASE is a freelance writer and editor who lives with his wife and three children in Monument, Colorado. He was a pastor for thirteen years, serving in Arkansas, Texas, and Colorado.

MARK TABB is general editor of the TH1NK REFERENCE COLLECTION, as well as the author of twelve books, including *Living with Less* and *Greater Than: Unconventional Thoughts on the Infinite God*. He and his family live in Indiana with their two dachshunds.

About the Scholar Board

All books in the TH1NK REFERENCE COLLECTION have been reviewed for biblical accuracy by the following academic scholars:

Robert Don Hughes, PhD

professor of missions and evangelism, Clear Creek Baptist College, Pineville, Kentucky

Bob has a strong pastoral background as well as great strength as a writer. He knows people. He knows their needs. He is on this board to make sure these books speak to real people in the real world. In addition, he has impeccable academic qualifications and understands and works well with those from across the theological scale.

Jerry A. Johnson, PhD

president and professor of theology and ethics, The Criswell College, Dallas, Texas

Jerry has extensive expertise in the area of theology and worldviews. In addition to serving as president of The Criswell College and as a theology professor there, he has a daily radio program that focuses on applying a Christian worldview to every aspect of life.

Keith Reeves, PhD

professor of New Testament and early Christian literature in the School of Theology, Azusa Pacific University, Azusa, California

Keith brings a different perspective to the books, from both a theological and geographical standpoint. His views on the Bible and creation differ from the others on the scholar board. Also, the fact that he teaches in Southern California gives him a different perspective from both the writers of the first three books and the members of the board. In addition, Keith is an expert in New Testament and early Christian literature.

Joseph Thomas, PhD

assistant professor of church history, Biblical Seminary, Hatfield, Pennsylvania; director of Christian History Institute (CHI)

Joe combines a strong background in church history with a Wesleyan/Holiness theological background. Before pursuing his PhD, he taught history in a Christian high school for eight years, thereby developing a strong ability to communicate with our target audience.

GET THE FULL THINK STUDENT LIBRARY.